ISBN 978-0-265-85588-1
PIBN 10899937

Marketing Research Report No 958

HOMEMAKERS' OPINIONS ABOUT FIBERS IN SELECTED HOUSEHOLD ITEMS:
A Nationwide Survey

U S Department of Agriculture • Statistical Reporting Service

Historic, archived document

Do not assume content reflects current
scientific knowledge, policies, or practices.

hou
Sur
(SR
to
woo
bas

Wei

PREFACE

This report concerns homemakers' attitudes toward fibers in selected household products. It is one of a group of studies conducted by the Special Surveys Branch, Standards and Research Division, Statistical Reporting Service (SRS), U.S. Department of Agriculture (USDA), to determine consumer reactions to agricultural products. The study was designed to provide the cotton and wool industries and USDA with guidelines for product research and improvement based on expressed consumer needs.

The study was conducted under the general direction of Margaret Weidenhamer, Chief, Special Surveys Branch, SRS. Advice was provided in the planning stage by subject matter specialists in USDA, the National Cotton Council of America, and The Wool Bureau, Inc. National Analysts, Inc., Philadelphia, Pa., under contract with USDA, collected the data.

CONTENTS

Washington, D.C. 20250

HIGHLIGHTS

When homemakers shop for household textile items, durability and ease of care are their chief considerations, according to a nationwide consumer survey conducted by the U.S. Department of Agriculture in the fall of 1969. Items focused on in the survey were sheets, blankets, room-size rugs, tablecloths, bedspreads, scatter rugs, draperies, curtains, and yard goods for home sewing.

Sheets

All cotton sheets were used in a majority of the households in the 12 months prior to the interview. About half the respondents said they had acquired new sheets in the past year, mainly by actual purchase rather than as gifts. A majority of those obtaining sheets during this time acquired three or more. Homemakers considered ease of care in a sheet more important than "that it be made of a certain fiber," judging by the higher ratings given durable press finish, regardless of fiber, and the fact that few respondents said they sent their sheets to a commercial laundry.

Blankets

Almost every homemaker reported having used some type of blanket in the past year--mainly blankets of all cotton or all wool. "Can be washed," "does not shrink," and "lasts a long time" were foremost in the respondents' minds when purchasing blankets. When rating the three major blanket fibers--all wool, all cotton, and all synthetic--homemakers gave wool the lowest rating. Although wool was considered durable, it was criticized by some homemakers because it "must not be washed" and it "shrinks."

Bedspreads

Most homemakers reported using bedspreads in the past year. Of the three types--chenille, tailored, and woven--chenille was most likely to be used. Cotton was mentioned as the fiber preferred and used most frequently, chiefly because it was easy to care for and durable. However, cotton chenille bedspreads were criticized by some because they formed lint.

Rugs

Area Rugs

Area or room-size rugs were used in about half the homes surveyed. These rugs, principally all wool, all nylon, or all acrylic, were used mainly in the living room and bedroom. All acrylic, all nylon, and all wool were the preferred fibers. They were said to "look good for a long time" and to be "easy to care for on a day-to-day basis." These characteristics were also major purchase considerations in addition to "ease of stain removal."

Scatter Rugs

Over three-fourths of the homemakers reported using scatter rugs in the home. Although these rugs were used by a majority of the homemakers in virtually every major room in the home except the dining room, over two-thirds of the respondents said they had used them in the bathroom. Fiber ratings in scatter rugs varied by their location--all acrylic received the highest rating for bedrooms and all cotton for bathrooms. Cotton scatter rugs, cited for their care and laundering characteristics, were criticized for their tendency to slide and wear out quickly.

Window Hangings

Draperies were used by a majority of the homemakers in the living room or bedroom. Curtains were more popular in kitchens and bedrooms.

Fiberglas was reported used and preferred by the highest proportion of homemakers for living room draperies. Nevertheless, about equal percentages of homemakers reported having used all nylon, all cotton, and all Fiberglas curtains in the living room in the past year.

When homemakers were questioned about the use of cotton curtains and/or draperies, the principal advantages and disadvantages reported were related to care and durability.

Tablecloths

A large majority of the respondents said they had used cloth tablecloths in the past year. Cotton (53 percent) and linen (22 percent) were the only fibers mentioned with any degree of frequency. Very few respondents (16 percent) reported using tablecloths with a special finish. When questioned, however, on their relative preference for these finishes, homemakers gave both durable press and stain resistance very high ratings.

The preference for special finishes was validated when respondents were asked to select those characteristics considered important in purchasing tablecloths: "easy to remove stains" and "looks good without ironing" were selected by better than half the homemakers.

Yard Goods

Almost half (45 percent) of the homemakers interviewed had purchased yard goods in the past year, primarily to be made into clothing for children 6-8 years of age and adults. Cotton was the leading fabric reported purchased, regardless of intended end use.

Summary table 1.—Homemakers' usage patterns, ratings, and purchase criteria of household textiles

End use	Percentage using	Major fiber and type used	Fibers and types rated highest	Purchase criteria
Sheets	100	All cotton regular	All cotton Polyester and cotton durable press	Lasts a long time Easy to wash Looks good without ironing Good value for the money
Blankets	98	All cotton regular All wool regular	All synthetic regular	Can be washed Does not shrink Lasts a long time Good value for the money
Bedspreads	96	Cotton chenille	Cotton durable press Cotton chenille	---
Room-size rugs	50	All wool	Living Room — All acrylic, All nylon, All wool Bedroom — All acrylic, All nylon	Living Room – Bedroom Looks good for a long time Easy to care for on a day-to-day basis Easy to remove stains
Scatter rugs	80	---	Bath — All cotton, All acrylic Bedroom — All acrylic, All nylon	
Draperies	80	Living Room Fiberglas	Living Room Fiberglas	
Curtains	89	Living Room Nylon, Fiberglas, Cotton	Living Room Fiberglas, Polyester	
Tablecloths	74	Cotton	Linen Cotton Durable press Stain resistant	Easy to remove stains Looks good without ironing Resists staining

Summary table 2.—Homemakers' opinions of major characteristics of fibers and finishes.

End use	Cotton	Polyester and cotton	Durable press cotton and durable press polyester and cotton	Wool	All synthetic
Sheets	Can be bleached, Easy to wash, Lasts a long time	Easy to wash, Looks good without ironing, Easy to dry	Looks good without ironing, Easy to wash, Easy to dry	---	---
Blankets	Can be washed, Good for use all year, Can buy it on sale	---	---	Lasts a long time, Shrinks, Not good for use all year, Must not be washed	Can be washed, Good for use all year, Colors stay like new, Good range of colors
Bedspreads	Easy to wash, Lasts a long time	---	---	---	---
Room-size rugs	Does not look good for a long time, Tends to mat or crush easily, Good range of colors, Easy to remove stains	---	---	Looks good for a long time, Difficult to remove stains, Good range of colors, Good value for the money	Easy to remove stains, Easy to care for on a day-to-day basis, Looks good for a long time, Good range of colors *(Nylon and acrylic)*
Scatter rugs	Easy to wash, Can be washed, Tends to slide				

vi

INTRODUCTION

In recent years the use of manmade fibers and blends of manmade and natural fibers in household products has reduced the share previously held by natural fibers in the U.S. market. The major purpose of this study is to provide information on beliefs and attitudes of homemakers toward natural fibers and synthetics as they affect the purchase of specific household products.

The survey reported here was conducted between October and December 1969 among 2,489 homemakers. These homemakers represented a cross section of private households located in both urban and rural areas throughout the 48 conterminous States. Respondents were selected entirely by area probability sampling procedures. The eligible respondent was defined as that person in the household with principal responsibility for the purchase and/or care of household furnishings. This definition permitted some male respondents to be included in the study. For reporting convenience, however, terms such as "homemakers" and "women" are used in this report to refer to all respondents, regardless of sex.

To ensure a satisfactory completion rate a differential callback procedure was employed. Urban households--where initial contact was not made--were revisited at least three times (either during different times of the same day or on different days) and rural households were revisited at least twice. These efforts resulted in an overall completion rate of 75 percent. A complete description of the sampling procedures used and estimates of sampling error for this survey are presented in the appendix.

1/ Mrs. Clayton is with the Special Surveys Branch, Standards and Research Division, Statistical Reporting Service, U.S. Department of Agriculture. Mrs. Sherman is with National Analysts, Inc., Philadelphia, Pa.

Areas of Questioning

The textile items included in this study were sheets, blankets, bedspreads, area or room-sized rugs, scatter rugs, draperies and curtains, tablecloths, and yard goods for home sewing. For each of these eight end products, use or nonuse in the past 12 months was ascertained. The desirability of selected fibers in each end product was investigated for all but yard goods. To obtain some indication of the respondent's attitudes toward various fibers, finishes, and types in specific household articles, homemakers were asked to indicate their opinion of each on a five-point scale, even if they had not used the item.

The relative importance of selected criteria in the purchase of sheets, blankets, area rugs, and tablecloths was determined. Women were asked to indicate whether sheets, blankets, and area rugs made of selected fibers and fiber combinations possess these characteristics. The perceived advantages and disadvantages of specific fibers were probed for bedspreads, scatter rugs, draperies and curtains, and tablecloths. In addition to the above, respondents were asked if they had acquired any sheets in the past 12 months and how their sheets were usually laundered. Finally, the interviewer determined the fiber, size, and price of the most recently purchased room-size rugs. The questionnaire used in this study is reproduced in the appendix.

Interpretation of Data

This survey relates to findings derived from a sample of the population, rather than a census of the total population. As such, it is subject to possible sample variations. The size of each subpopulation, sampling error for four items, and approximate confidence limits for other percentages generated by this study are shown in the appendix.

The findings are presented as summaries of the statements made by the homemakers and are subject to any errors they made in reporting their beliefs and attitudes. It is especially important to keep this factor in mind in analyzing data on fiber experience and preference, since difficulties with fiber identification have some influence on the validity of respondent's statements. Inadvertent misstatements by respondents may occur because of oversights, lack of information, or confusion about fiber content. There are many kinds of fibers and fiber combinations on the market, and problems of identification may arise from the use of descriptive or brand names for a product. Furthermore, household items made of such mixtures as polyester and cotton, for example, may have been identified as either polyester or cotton. There may have been confusion among such fibers as rayon, acetate, polyester, and nylon also. However, since this study was not intended to provide estimates of fiber consumption but rather to collect data about the attitudes and impressions homemakers hold toward the various fibers, the statements made were accepted as given.

Since respondents were also describing from memory the number of items and the fibers they owned, made, or bought, some forgetting, overstatement, or misunderstanding may have crept into the responses. No inventory of household furnishings was conducted.

Throughout the questionnaire the word "fiber" was used; more familiar terms such as "material" or "fabric" were generally avoided, with the exception of questions on home sewing. Care was taken in the section on sheets to point out to the homemaker that the terms "muslin" and "percale" refer to weave and not to fiber. Throughout this report, "rayon" is occasionally used for the category "rayon/acetate."

Text Tabulations

Summary tabulations are included throughout the text. Some percentages have been presented which do not add to 100, and some subcategories do not equal the percentage for an entire category. This occurs because only highlights are presented in such tables. Multiple responses account for tables adding to more than 100 percent and for subcategories adding to more than percentages shown for an entire category. All percentages are based on the total sample of 2,489, except as noted.

The proportions of respondents who rated a product as either "1--not a very good choice for me" or "5--a very good choice for me" are shown in the text. This represents both ends of the 5-point scale used to show the acceptability of selected fibers or selected characteristics for a given end product, if respondents were buying a specific end product at that time.

Respondents were asked to indicate total annual household income before taxes. Households were then classified in approximately equal-sized groups as follows:

Group	Income	Households reporting
Lower	Under $6,000	822
Middle	$6,000-$9,999	731
Upper	$10,000 or more	722

A total of 214 respondents did not answer the income question.

Respondents were also classified according to age, education, and size of household. Throughout the report, the terms "family" and "household" are used interchangeably.

The discussion in the text focuses on those results that appeared to contribute most to an understanding of homemakers' opinions about the subject areas covered in this study. Therefore, responses to a few questions have not been included in the text or appendix tables. (The references in parentheses are to the numbered questions in the questionnaire and to the appendix tables which summarize answers to the questionnaire.)

Data are discussed with reference to demographic characteristics when results are of particular interest. For more comprehensive coverage, the reader is directed to the appendix tables. Findings by background characteristics are solely descriptive in nature. The reader is cautioned against assigning any cause-and-effect relationship from these results. Highly interrelated personal characteristics, such as age, education, and income levels, are shown separately. Combining them would have resulted in an excessive number of separate groups with too few respondents in each. However, tables showing the interrelationship among characteristics are shown in the appendix.

SHEETS

Usage: Fibers and Types

Forty-six percent of the respondents reported they had acquired new sheets in the preceding year. Of these, more than half indicated they had obtained three or more during this time. A majority said they had actually purchased the sheets; only a few indicated they were received as gifts. Respondents who had acquired sheets in the past year were more likely to be younger, better educated, have larger families composed of children and adults, and have higher family incomes. About a third (34 percent) of all the respondents said that their last acquisition of sheets was 1 to 3 years prior to the interview, while about a fifth (19 percent) indicated that it had been over 3 years.

Better than 8 in 10 homemakers said they had used cotton sheets in the year preceding the interview, with a majority indicating the use of regular all cotton sheets; only about 1 in 10 said they had used durable press all cotton sheets. The use of polyester and cotton blend durable press sheets was reported by only 14 percent; an even smaller percentage (10 percent) indicated using regular polyester and cotton (not durable press).

The use of durable press sheets was more characteristic of younger, better educated, more urbanized homemakers as well as those with larger families. Older homemakers and those living in the South were more likely to have used cotton sheets in their homes in the previous 12 months.

(Questions 1-9)

Fiber and Finish Ratings

Despite far more widespread ownership of regular all cotton sheets, two other types of sheets--durable press all cotton and durable press cotton with polyester--rated on a par with all cotton. Better than 4 in 10 homemakers gave a rating of "5--a very good choice for me" to three of the four types of sheets being considered. They were all cotton, durable press all cotton, and durable press cotton with polyester. About half as many respondents gave this rating to the fourth type, regular polyester and cotton blend sheets. However, about 1 in 10 homemakers gave all four sheets a rating of "1--not a very good choice for me."

4

Ratings	Polyester and cotton	All cotton	Durable press polyester and cotton	Durable press cotton
	----------------------------------Percent----------------------------			
5	27	47	45	42
1	12	11	10	8

(Question 10)

Major Factors in Purchasing Sheets

Respondents were presented with a card listing 15 attributes which might be used· to characterize sheets and asked to select those ideas which would be most important to them if they were buying sheets. They were encouraged to select as many as they felt important. The intent of this question was to gain insight into factors which influence the purchase of sheets in general.

Durability was selected by the largest percentage of homemakers as an important factor when purchasing sheets. "Easy to wash," "looks good without ironing," and "good value for the money" were selected by nearly equal percentages of homemakers and ranked second to durability in importance.

Relatively few respondents said that a certain fiber or weave was an important consideration when purchasing sheets.

The following tabulation lists the characteristics selected by the homemakers as most important in the purchase of sheets:

	Percent
Lasts a long time	63
Easy to wash	57
Looks good without ironing	55
Good value for the money	55
Keeps its whiteness or color for a long time	48
Can be bleached	33
Easy to remove stains	31
Smooth to the touch	29
Can buy it on sale	28
Easy to dry	27
Made of a certain fiber: cotton, etc.	18
A certain weave: muslin or percale	17
Good range of colors or prints	16
Does not "pill"	13
Absorbent	5

(Question 11)

Characteristics of Specific Fibers and Finishes in Sheets

Having indicated the characteristics they considered most important in purchasing sheets, respondents were then presented with a card (Card D) which listed 13 pairs of attributes that might apply to specific kinds of sheets. Each pair reflected both the positive and negative aspect of that attribute. Respondents were asked to select from this list those phrases that described their opinions about the four selected fiber and finish combinations: all cotton and polyester-cotton blend, with and without a durable press finish. It was anticipated that such a procedure would give further insight into the factors that might influence a homemaker's purchase of specific sheets.

All cotton sheets were mainly characterized as durable, easy to wash, and bleachable. Other frequently mentioned attributes of regular all cotton, which were generally not shared by the other kinds of sheets, were "can buy on sale," "good value for the money," "keeps its whiteness," and "easy to remove stains." The only negative attribute that appeared with any degree of frequency was that all cotton does not look good without ironing.

Of the homemakers interviewed about 1 in 4 said they did not know or had no opinion about sheets of polyester and cotton blends and those with a durable press finish. When respondents did venture an opinion about these sheets, they were more likely to characterize them as "looks good without ironing" (a characteristic mainly attributed to durable press), "easy to wash," "easy to dry," "smooth to the touch," and "lasts a long time."

The following tabulation shows the percentage of all women selecting positive and negative characteristics of the four kinds of sheets discussed:

| | Regular | | Durable Press | |
	Polyester--cotton blend	All cotton	Polyester--cotton blend	All cotton
	----------------Percent----------------			
Lasts a long time	34	60	27	32
Wears out rather quickly	5	6	6	5
Easy to wash	50	63	46	47
Not easy to wash	1	2	1	1
Looks good without ironing	46	14	60	54
Does not look good without ironing	7	38	2	5
Good value for the money	21	43	20	23
Not good value for the money	4	2	4	3
Keeps whiteness/color long time	21	40	17	21
Does not keep whiteness/color long time	9	6	8	5

6

	Regular		Durable Press	
	Polyester-- cotton blend	All cotton	Polyester-- cotton blend	All cotton
	----------------Percent----------------			
Can be bleached	11	64	8	17
Must not be bleached	16	1	18	10
Easy to remove stains	15	38	12	16
Difficult to remove stains	9	7	11	8
Smooth to the touch	31	21	37	31
Rough to the touch	1	14	1	3
Can buy on sale	19	47	17	19
Cannot buy on sale	3	*	4	4
Easy to dry	42	28	43	39
Not easy to dry	1	12	1	2
Good range of colors/prints	21	28	22	22
Not good range of colors/prints	1	2	1	*
Does not "pill"	11	19	11	12
"Pills"	5	3	4	3
Absorbent	7	23	6	11
Not absorbent	7	1	9	6
Don't know, no opinion	23	2	24	24
Total favorable mentions	329	488	326	344
Total unfavorable mentions	69	94	70	55

* Less than 1 percent

(Questions 12, 13, 14 and 15)

Laundering Procedures

The importance of care consideration in the selection of sheets is underscored by the fact that relatively few homemakers said that they sent their sheets to a commercial laundry. The vast majority washed their own sheets, either at home or in a laundermat.

Drying methods, however, varied considerably more. Over a third of the respondents said that their sheets "dry on the clothesline;" about a fourth machine dry them; a like proportion indicated that either they machine dry their sheets or dry them on the clothesline, depending on the weather.

(Question 16)

BLANKETS

Usage: Fibers and Types

Almost every homemaker reported using blankets in the past year. Use of
more than one type (thermal, electric, and regular) was not uncommon. A large
majority of all segments of the population reported the use of regular blankets
in the past year--principally, all cotton, all wool, and all synthetic.

Much smaller proportions indicated that they had used thermal or electric
blankets. All synthetic and all cotton were the fibers reported most frequently
However, only 5 percent of the respondents reported having used all cotton
electric blankets in the past year. The use of thermal and electric blankets
was reported by somewhat larger percentages of the better educated homemakers
and those with larger family incomes. Younger homemakers and those with large
families were more likely to have used thermal blankets; conversely, larger
percentages of older homemakers and those with smaller families indicated the
use of electric blankets in the past year.

The following tabulation shows the percentage of women reporting the use
of blankets by major fibers and types:

		Percent	
Used blankets of some kind	98		
Used regular blankets		89	
All cotton			44
All wool			40
All synthetic			33
Used thermal blankets		38	
All synthetic			16
All cotton			13
Used electric blankets		28	
All synthetic			14
All cotton			5
All wool			4
Did not use	2		

(Questions 22 and 23)

Fiber and Finish Ratings

Homemakers were asked to rate three different fibers (all wool, all cotton,
and all synthetic) and three different types of blankets (regular, electric,
and thermal). About one-fourth gave a rating of "5--a very good choice for
me" to all three fibers. However, the attitudes of many homemakers toward these
fibers was more realistically represented by the proportion who rated the
fibers "1--not a very good choice for me." Less than one-fourth gave this
rating to all cotton and all synthetic, while almost one-half indicated that
wool was "not a very good choice" for them. Ratings of all three types of

8

blankets were somewhat similar, with electric blankets being the least popular.

Rating	Synthetic	Cotton	Wool	Regular	Thermal	Electric
	------------------------------Percent------------------------------					
5	27	24	25	36	35	27
1	17	23	43	10	21	43

(Question 17)

Major Factors in Blanket Purchases

As with sheets, homemakers were presented with a card of selected attributes and asked to indicate those they considered most important in purchasing
blankets. Washability was the chief consideration for most respondents. Over
half the homemakers were also concerned with whether the blanket would shrink
and if it would last a long time. Good value for the money was important to
about half the respondents; however, only about one-fifth said "can buy it on
sale" was a major factor.

Performance is apparently more important to blanket purchasers than fiber
content. Only about one-fourth of those interviewed said that the fact that
a blanket is "made of a certain fiber" was a major purchase consideration.

The attributes and their frequency of mention are:

	Percent
Can be washed	84
Does not shrink	68
Lasts a long time	60
Good value for the money	50
Colors stay like new	43
Good for use all year round	39
Does not stretch	37
Does not "pill"	34
Made of a certain fiber: cotton, etc.	28
Easy to remove stains	26
Does not burn easily	22
Can buy it on sale	21
Good range of colors	20

(Question 18)

9

Characteristics of Specific Fibers in Blankets

Synthetic blankets, characterized mainly as washable, were not as familiar to the respondents as cotton and wool. One-fifth of the respondents did not select any of the listed positive or negative phrases as indicative of their opinions of synthetic blankets. Cotton, considered washable by a vast majority of the homemakers, was also characterized as "good for use all year," "can buy it on sale," "easy to remove stains," and "does not shrink." Wool, although characterized as durable more often than cotton or synthetic blankets, was more likely to be criticized because it "must not be washed," "shrinks," and is "not good for use all year round."

The following tabulation shows the percentages of women selecting positive and negative characteristics describing each of the three kinds of blankets discussed:

	Wool	Cotton	Synthetic
	--------------Percent--------------		
Can be washed	26	85	61
Must not be washed	44	*	3
Does not shrink	11	37	33
Shrinks	52	14	6
Lasts a long time	58	34	34
Wears out rather quickly	2	19	6
Good value for the money	32	33	30
Not good value for the money	7	7	4
Colors stay like new	33	25	36
Colors do not stay like new	5	13	3
Good for use all year round	9	46	38
Not good for use all year round	45	12	5
Does not stretch	19	23	22
Stretches	7	9	7
Does not "pill"	13	14	12
"Pills"	22	16	17
Easy to remove stains	7	37	16
Difficult to remove stains	27	3	10
Does not burn easily	10	9	9
Burns easily	13	9	11
Can buy it on sale	20	39	26
Cannot buy it on sale	4	1	1

	Wool	Cotton	Synthetic
	-------------Percent-------------		
Good range of colors	28	31	35
Not a good range of colors	2	2	1
Don't know, no opinion	4	5	20
Total favorable mentions	266	413	352
Total unfavorable mentions	230	105	74

* Less than 1 percent   (Questions 19, 20, and 21)

BEDSPREADS

Usage: Fibers and Types

As with blankets, nearly every homemaker (96 percent) reported the use of some type of bedspread in the year prior to the interview. The introduction to this section of the questionnaire read: "The bedspread industry separates bedspreads into three types. In addition to the tufted or chenille bedspread, a second type is the woven. This type is made of material woven mainly for bedspreads. It is generally heavier and the pattern or color is woven through, not printed on. It has almost the same pattern on both sides except the colors are reversed. All other bedspreads are called tailored. These are made of material that could be used for other items. They may be quilted, flat or ruffled, fitted or not." The largest majority (69 percent) said they had used chenille spreads. The use of tailored spreads was reported by 47 percent; least frequently mentioned were woven bedspreads (35 percent). For all three types of bedspreads the most frequently mentioned fiber was cotton. Chenille bedspreads were used by higher proportions of respondents who were less well educated and those with lower family incomes. Tailored and woven spreads, on the other hand, were used by higher proportions of the better educated home-makers and those with higher incomes.

The following tabulation summarizes reported usage of bedspreads by types and major fibers.

	Percent
Used bedspreads of some kind	96
Used chenille bedspreads	69
Cotton	63
Used tailored bedspreads	47
Cotton	24
Rayon/acetate	8
Used woven bedspreads	35
Cotton	27

(Questions 24-30)

11

Perceived Advantages and Disadvantages of Cotton Bedspreads

Cotton, regardless of type of bedspread, was the only fiber whose use in the 12 months prior to the interview was indicated by a high proportion of respondents. Perceived advantages and disadvantages volunteered by respondents who had used these bedspreads revealed that ease of care, durability, and appearance were important considerations in making cotton bedspreads widely acceptable. Regardless of style, cotton bedspreads were valued chiefly because they can be washed easily and last a long time.

Cotton chenille was the only type of bedspread which generated a significant disadvantage. Almost 4 in 10 users said that cotton chenille bedspreads formed lint; about the same proportion, however, said these spreads had no disadvantages.

It should be noted that questions about advantages and disadvantages were asked only of those who said they had used a specific fiber and type of bedspread in the past year. In the appendix table, however, percentages were based upon the total number of all respondents.

The following tabulation summarizes the major advantages and disadvantages cited by users for the three types of cotton bedspreads:

	Cotton chenille	Cotton woven	Cotton tailored
	------------Percent 1/------------		
Advantages			
Easy to wash	35	26	23
Lasts a long time	28	30	19
Little or no ironing	22	19	12
Can be washed	21	22	25
Looks good after laundering	19	14	7
Easy to dry	14	8	8
Colors stay like new	13	21	12
Attractive, pretty	13	16	21
No advantages	2	1	3
Disadvantages			
Lints	36	2	1
No disadvantages	43	61	50

1/ Percentages are based on total number of respondents who had used that type/fiber bedspread.

(Questions 31 and 32)

Fiber and Finish Ratings

Homemakers were presented with a list of eight different kinds of bed-spreads and asked to rate them. They comprised four fibers (polyester and cotton, polyester, cotton, and rayon); three types (chenille, woven, and tailored); and one fabric finish, durable press. All cotton was clearly the most popular fiber, with about half the respondents giving it a rating of "5--a very good choice for me." On the other hand, rayon, the least popular, was rated "1--not a very good choice for me" by similar proportions.

Homemakers' opinions of types of spreads are somewhat less definitive. Although chenille received more negative votes than the other two types, it also was characterized more often as "5--a very good choice for me."

Durable press finish was given a "5" rating by almost half the respondents.

Rating	Polyester and cotton	Polyester	Cotton	Rayon	Chenille	Woven	Tailored	Durable press
				Percent				
5	27	23	51	6	42	31	34	47
1	11	15	9	48	20	15	15	9

(Question 33)

RUGS

Usage: Fibers and Types

Two types of rugs were considered in this study: area or room-size rugs (defined as larger than 4 x 6 feet but not wall-to-wall) and scatter rugs (defined as no larger than 4 x 6).

Scatter rugs were more widely used than area rugs, according to the home-makers interviewed. A large majority (80 percent) said they had used scatter rugs in the past year, while only about half indicated the use of area rugs in their homes during this time. Nearly half the respondents who used area rugs had purchased at least one within the past 3 years, mainly for the living room or bedroom. All wool, all nylon, all acrylic, and all cotton were mentioned, in that order, as the fibers most recently purchased in area rugs. Scatter rugs were used in every major room in the house except the dining room by more than one-third of the homemakers; almost two-thirds indicated they used scatter rugs in their bathrooms.

Homemakers in the Northeast were more likely than those in other regions to have used area rugs and to have purchased a wool one most recently. The use of scatter rugs, while dominant in all segments of the population, was more likely in homes in the West and North Central section of the country.

(Questions 42-45)

(Questions 52,53)

13

Fiber and Finish Ratings

Room-Size Rugs

In purchasing a room-size rug for either the bedroom or living room, the homemakers interviewed said they would be more likely to choose an all acrylic or all nylon rug rather than an all cotton one. How they rated wool depended on whether the rug was intended for the living room or bedroom. All wool was given the highest rating by more than a third of the respondents for use in the living room, but by only a fourth for use in the bedroom. On the negative side, about a third of the homemakers interviewed rated wool "1--not a very good choice for me" for use in the bedroom and about a fourth gave it the same rating for use in the living room.

	Rating	All wool	All acrylic	Cotton	Nylon
		------------------------------Percent------------------------------			
Bedroom	5	26	34	12	32
	1	35	12	42	17
Living room	5	37	34	7	33
	1	28	11	56	19

(Questions 34,35)

Major Factors in Room-Size Rug Purchases

Whether for use in the living room or the bedroom, the major considerations in purchasing an area rug were appearance over time, ease of care on a day-to-day basis, and ease of stain removal. Homemakers considered durability without loss of initial appearance of great importance in selecting area rugs, particularly for the living room. Ease of care on a day-to-day basis was slightly less important than durability in appearance in the purchase of a living room rug. Both were equally important factors in the purchase of an area bedroom rug, however. A majority of homemakers selected ease of stain removal as an important consideration when purchasing a rug for either the living room or the bedroom.

The following tabulation shows the percentage of homemakers who selected each of the following characteristics as an important purchase consideration when buying area rugs:

	Bedroom	Living Room
	--------Percent---------	
Looks good for a long time	68	73
Easy to care for on a day-to-day basis	68	68
Easy to remove stains	57	68
Does not "fuzz" or shed	51	46
Good value for the money	46	45
Good in homes where there are children	39	41
Does not mat down or crush easily	38	44

14

	Bedroom	Living Room
	--------Percent--------	
Made of a certain fiber: wool, etc.	33	36
Good range of colors	32	36
Does not burn easily	26	27
Little or no static electricity	23	24

(Questions 36 and 37)

Characteristics of Specific Fibers in Room-Size Rugs

Homemakers' opinions that both acrylic and nylon fibers possess those characteristics which they consider most important in purchasing area rugs appear to account for the higher ratings accorded these fibers. Although wool excelled in durability in appearance, stain removal was considered more difficult with wool then with the synthetic fibers. To a lesser extent, wool was also judged more difficult to care for on a day-to-day basis. The attributes on which acrylic and nylon rated well were mentioned by homemakers as often as durability in appearance when fiber was considered in the selection of an area rug.

The homemaker's attitude toward cotton in area rugs is reflected in the small proportion selecting positive factors to characterize this fiber. Cotton area rugs were criticized most often for crushing or matting down easily and for failing to "look good for a long time." The only positive factors mentioned by as many as one-fourth of the respondents were "easy to remove stains" and "good range of colors." However, about a fifth of the homemakers criticized cotton because of difficulty in removing stains.

The following tabulation shows the percentage of women selecting positive and negative characteristics associated with each of the four rug fibers:

	Acrylic	Nylon	Wool	Cotton
	-------------Percent-------------			
Looks good for a long time	36	44	52	12
Does not look good for a long time	6	7	8	36
Easy to care for on a day-to-day basis	41	46	30	20
Difficult to care for on a day-to-day basis	4	6	21	24
Easy to remove stains	45	52	15	27
Difficult to remove stains	6	7	41	21
Does not "fuzz" or shed	19	23	21	12
Tends to "fuzz" or shed	10	10	20	19

15

	Acrylic	Nylon	Wool	Cotton
	---------------Percent---------------			
Good value for the money	27	33	35	19
Not a good value for the money	3	4	7	19
Good in homes where there are children	33	39	16	20
Not good in homes where there are children	4	6	27	18
Does not mat down or crush easily	20	24	28	6
Tends to mat down or crush easily	8	10	12	30
Good range of colors	36	39	37	28
Not good range of colors	1	1	2	2
Does not burn easily	11	11	12	8
Burns easily	8	13	14	13
Little or no static electricity	11	9	18	22
A lot of static electricity	10	23	12	2
Don't know, no opinion	28	17	10	17
Total favorable mentions	279	320	264	174
Total unfavorable mentions	60	87	164	184

(Questions 38-41)

Fibers in Area Rugs Purchased Most Recently

According to the testimony of homemakers interviewed in this study, wool area rugs have decreased in popularity, while cotton and synthetics, especially acrylics, are on the upswing.

The following table summarizes the percentages of homemakers who reported acrylic, nylon, wool, or cotton as the fiber content of the last area rug purchased and still in use when no time restrictions were imposed and when such purchases were confined to the 3 years prior to the interview. In each instance in this tabulation, the base is the number of homemakers who had purchased area rugs for that time period.

	Most recent purchase	Most recent purchases in the 3 years prior to interview
	----------Percent------------	
Wool	29	18
Nylon	20	24
Acrylic	14	24
Cotton	12	17
Number of cases	1,058	511

(Questions 44 and 45)

Price paid per square yard for purchases in the past 3 years ranged from a low of less than $2.25 to a high of over $14.25. On the average, cotton was the cheapest and wool the most expensive. The following tabulation summarizes homemakers' responses by fiber and reported cost per square yard for the last area rug purchased in the 3 years prior to the interview:

	Acrylic	Nylon	Wool	Cotton
	---------------Number----------------			
Less than $2.25	16	13	9	30
$2.25 - $3.25	7	12	8	14
$3.26 - $4.00	14	17	3	13
$4.01 - $5.00	8	22	6	14
$5.01 - $6.50	23	19	7	6
$6.51 - $8.25	12	14	12	6
$8.26 - $10.25	15	12	10	1
$10.26 - $14.25	10	7	9	1
$14.26 or more	10	-	27	-
Don't know, don't remember	10	6	3	3
Number of rugs	125	122	94	88
	-------------Dollars---------------			
Reported average price per square yard	6.89	5.20	14.22	3.33

(Questions 45-47)

17

Fiber and Finish Ratings

Scatter Rugs

Synthetic scatter rugs (all acrylic or nylon) were equally acceptable for either bedroom or bathroom, according to homemakers' ratings. Rayon, on the other hand, was generally considered unacceptable for either use.

Homemakers' attitudes toward scatter rugs made of wool or cotton varied according to their intended use. Cotton scatter rugs in the bedroom received about as many negative as positive ratings. However, when intended for the bathroom, cotton scatter rugs led the list; three times as many respondents rated them "5--a very good choice for me" as "1--not a very good choice for me."

On the other hand, wool was rejected as a bathroom scatter rug by an overwhelming majority of the homemakers (80 percent). As a scatter rug in the bedroom, however, wool was more acceptable. About half rejected it, while a fifth gave it their highest rating.

	Bedroom				
	Wool	All acrylic	Cotton	Nylon	Rayon
Rating	----------------------------Percent----------------------------				
5	20	32	28	31	5
1	48	14	27	18	48

	Bathroom				
	Wool	All acrylic	Cotton	Nylon	Rayon
Rating	----------------------------Percent----------------------------				
5	4	31	44	31	5
1	80	17	15	19	50

(Questions 48,49)

18

Perceived Advantages and Disadvantages of Cotton Scatter Rugs

All homemakers were asked to cite the advantages and disadvantages of using cotton scatter rugs. Most of the perceived advantages centered around care and laundering characteristics. Major mentions in this area were "easy to wash," "can be washed," and "machine washable." The only other advantages mentioned by as many as 1 in 10 were "lasts a long time," "good range of colors," and "inexpensive." About a third of the homemakers said there were no disadvantages to cotton scatter rugs. The two-thirds who did feel that cotton scatter rugs left something to be desired were mainly concerned with their performance and durability. "Tends tc slide," "wears out rather quickly," "doesn't lie flat," and "colors do not stay like new" were the characteristics mentioned most often.

The following tabulation summarizes the major advantages and disadvantages attributed to use of cotton scatter rugs:

Advantages	Percent
Easy to wash	33
Can be washed	25
Machine washable	13
Lasts a long time	13
Inexpensive	12
Good range of colors	10
No advantages	9

Disadvantages	
Tends to slide	19
Wears out rather quickly	12
Doesn't lie flat	12
Colors do not stay like new	11
No disadvantages	31

(Questions 50 and 51)

WINDOW HANGINGS

Usage: Fibers and Types

This study focused on the use of two types of window hangings: draperies--"window hangings which are frequently made of heavier materials, and are generally more formal" -- and curtains--"less formal window hangings which are unlined, thinner materials, and often transparent." About 8 in 10 used draperies; 9 in 10 used curtains. Use of draperies increased as income, education, and size of family increased; however, homemakers in the Northeast and those 60 years of age and older were less likely to have used them in the preceding 12 months.

The use of curtains, on the other hand, did not vary appreciably by socioeconomic characteristics. Draperies, although used by a majority of homemakers in the living room or bedroom, could be found in 14 percent of the homemakers' kitchens. However, curtains were a more popular choice for kitchens and bedrooms. The following table shows reported use of draperies and curtains in specific rooms:

	Draperies	Curtains
	-------Percent---------	
Living room	76	34
Bedrooms	55	63
Kitchen	14	80

(Questions 54 and 57)

About 2 in 10 of the homemakers interviewed reported that their living room draperies were made of Fiberglas, while cotton and cotton-rayon blend draperies for the living room were each owned by about 1 in 10. Nylon, Fiberglas, cotton, and polyester were the most frequently reported living room curtains used.

The following tabulation summarizes the fibers reported used in living room draperies and curtains:

	Draperies	Curtains
	-------Percent---------	
Fiberglas	23	6
Cotton	13	6
Cotton and rayon/acetate blend	10	2
Rayon/acetate	5	2
Nylon	2	7
Polyester	1	5

(Questions 55 and 58)

adv

cha

Fiber and Finish Ratings

When asked to rate four selected fibers or blends, homemakers clearly indicated that Fiberglas was the most popular fiber for draperies. However, about a fifth gave this fiber the lowest rating as their choice for living room draperies. Rayon and cotton were both rated "1--not a very good choice for me" by about a third of the homemakers. However, cotton received a "5" rating from about a fourth of the respondents, while rayon was accorded this rating by only about 1 in 10.

20

Fiber and finish ratings for curtains were about the same as for draperies, although the homemaker was given six fibers or blends to rate instead of four--two additional synthetics, nylon and polyester, and cotton and polyester blend instead of cotton and rayon.

Draperies

Rating	Cotton	Rayon	Cotton and rayon	Fiberglas
	------------------------------Percent-------------------------------			
5	24	10	15	47
1	33	37	22	21

(Question 56)

Curtains

Rating	Cotton	Rayon	Fiberglas	Nylon	Polyester	Cotton and polyester
	------------------------------Percent-------------------------------					
5	23	6	45	29	31	20
1	39	45	23	18	11	14

(Question 59)

Advantages and Disadvantages in Using Cotton Draperies and Curtains

According to the comments volunteered by homemakers, both the principal advantages and disadvantages of cotton in draperies and curtains were related to care and durability. Cotton was valued for its washability and long-lasting characteristics, but its need for ironing and its tendency to fade were perceived as distinct disadvantages. Homemakers reporting no disadvantages in using cotton--26 percent--outnumbered those who said there were no advantages (19 percent).

21

The following tabulation summarizes the major advantages and di:
in the use of cotton draperies and curtains (reported by 5 percent o
all respondents).

	Percent
Advantages	
Can be washed	31
Easy to wash	20
Looks good after laundering	7
Lasts a long time	16
Colors stay like new	9
Good range of colors	10
Attractive, pretty	5
Inexpensive	11
No advantages	19
Disadvantages	
Requires ironing	34
Difficult to iron	7
Colors do not stay like new	16
Does not resist stain or soil	7
Wears out rather quickly	6
Shrinks	5
Not attractive, not pretty	8
No disadvantages	26

(Questions 6

TABLECLOTHS

Usage: Fiber and Finishes

A large majority (74 percent) of the respondents said they had
tablecloths during the previous year. However, 36 percent indicated
had used them only for special occasions.

Use of cloth tablecloths was reported by smaller proportions of
homemakers, the less well educated, those with lower family incomes,
makers under 30 years of age.

(Questions 6

22

About half of all homemakers (53 percent) reported having used cotton tablecloths in the past year; significantly fewer (22 percent) indicated the use of linen. No other fiber was mentioned by as many as 5 percent of the homemakers.

When asked if any of these tablecloths had special finishes to make them more convenient to use, a relatively small proportion (16 percent) replied in the affirmative. Durable press was the only finish mentioned by as many as 6 percent, with durable press cotton the only fiber-finish combination used by as many as 3 percent of the homemakers.

	Percent	
Did not use any tablecloth	26	
Did not use any tablecloth with a special finish	58	
Used a tablecloth with a special finish	16	
Durable press	6	
Cotton		3
Cotton and polyester		1
Polyester		1
Wash-and-wear	1	
Stain release	3	
Soil resistant	1	
Other special finish	*	
Don't know, no answer to finish	4	

---

* Less than 1 percent

The only advantage of tablecloths with a durable press finish mentioned with any degree of frequency by homemakers who had used them was that they required little or no ironing. However, when questioned about possible disadvantages of tablecloths with this finish, a majority said there were none.

(Questions 64-68)

Fiber and Finish Ratings

Fiber preference in tablecloths was much less clearly defined than home-makers' preferences for both durable press and stain resistant finishes in tablecloths. A majority indicated their interest by rating both finishes "5--a very good choice for me."

While both linen and cotton were rated "5" by high proportions of the homemakers, negative ratings of "1" were also given these fibers by significant proportions.

23

	Linen	Cotton	Polyester	Polyester and cotton	Cotton and rayon	Durable press	Stain and soil resistant
Rating	------	------	---------	----------Percent	--------	-----	-----------
5	40	30	22	21	7	60	73
1	20	15	12	10	29	7	3

(Question 70)

Major Factors in Purchasing Tablecloths

To the homemaker, major purchase considerations in buying cloth tablecloth were about the same as when purchasing sheets, blankets, and area rugs. However, the proportion selecting these factors as important varied for each product. "Easy to remove stains," "looks good without ironing," and "resists staining" were mentioned by half or more of the respondents as characteristics they considered important when purchasing cloth tablecloths. Of the factors listed, "made of a certain fiber" was of least concern to the respondents.

	Percent
Easy to remove stains	71
Looks good without ironing	59
Resists staining	50
Lasts a long time	48
Durable press finish	46
Easy to iron	40
Can be dried in a machine	39
Made of certain fiber: cotton, etc.	27

(Question 69)

YARD GOODS

Almost half (45 percent) of the respondents had purchased yard goods in the 12 months prior to the interview. Most of them (42 percent) said the yard goods were to be made into clothing, mainly for children 6-18 years of age and for adults. Those who indicated that they had purchased yard goods for items other than clothing (15 percent) mentioned a variety of articles as intended end products, but curtains or draperies predominated.

A majority of the purchasers of yard goods said they had bought cotton fabrics, whether the intended end products were clothing or items other than clothing. Only three other fabrics--wool, cotton and polyester blend, and all polyester--were mentioned by a sizable proportion of the homemakers. Each of these fabrics was mentioned primarily for clothing end products.

Homemakers who used yard goods for clothing reported that an average of eight clothing items had been made from fabric purchased in the year prior to the interview. Those who bought yard goods for other purposes had made about four items on the average.

Homemakers with larger families, higher family incomes, more education, and those from rural areas were more likely to report the purchase of yard goods. However, fewer respondents from the Northeast section of the country and those 50 years of age and older reported purchasing yard goods.

(Questions 71-79)

Sample Design

The sample was a stratified multistage random sample of all private households in the 48 conterminous States. In each household, the homemaker--the
person chiefly responsible for either buying or caring for sheets and other
household "linens" for the household--was interviewed. Usable interviews were
obtained from 2,489 homemakers.

The structure of the sample, with reference to the first-stage sampling
units (FSU's), is indicated by the following table which shows the number of
first-stage units in the sample by geographic area and zones.

Geographic region and division	Zone 1	Zone 2	Zone 3	Total
	---------------------Number---------------------			
Northeast:				
New England............:	2	2	2	6
Middle Atlantic........:	12	7	5	24
North Central:				
East North Central.....:	8	6	6	20
West North Central.....:	2	2	6	10
South:				
South Atlantic.........:	2	3	7	12
East South Central.....:	2	1	4	7
West South Central.....:	4	1	4	9
West:				
Mountain...............:	2	1	2	5
Pacific................:	6	5	2	13
Total..............:	40	28	38	106

The nine geographic areas correspond to the nine census divisions, except
that Maryland, Delaware, and Washington, D.C., metropolitan areas were included
in the Middle Atlantic division rather than in the South Atlantic. Within
each of the nine divisions, three groupings or zones were used as follows:

Zone 1 -- That portion of a Standard Metropolitan Statistical
Area (SMSA) containing one or more cities of 50,000
or more inhabitants.

Zone 2 -- Portions of SMSA's not included in Zone 1. These
consist primarily of suburban communities but may
also include rural territory within an SMSA boundary.

Zone 3 -- Non-SMSA areas consisting of small towns and rural
farm and nonfarm territory.

Each zone within each division was further divided, giving a total of 106
strata of approximately equal size. A primary sampling unit (PSU) in Zone 1
was a city or a major subdivision of a city, and in Zones 2 and 3 was a county
or noncity portion of a county. All land area in the 48 States was assigned
to a PSU, and one PSU was drawn with probability proportional to size from
each of the 106 strata. Since the objective was to have each FSU contain
approximately 10,000 households, the 106 selected PSU's were divided into
area FSU's of approximately 10,000 households. In PSU's involving cities where
census tracts exist, such tracts were combined to form FSU's. In nontracted
areas, Census Enumeration Districts were combined to form FSU's. From each of
the PSU's, one FSU was drawn, again with the probability in proportion to size.

Listing of States in Each Region

Northeast	North Central	South	West
Maine	Ohio	North Carolina	Montana
New Hampshire	Michigan	South Carolina	Arizona
Vermont	Indiana	Virginia	Colorado
Massachusetts	Illinois	Georgia	Idaho
Rhode Island	Wisconsin	Florida	Wyoming
Connecticut	Minnesota	West Virginia	Utah
New York	Iowa	Arkansas	Nevada
New Jersey	Missouri	Louisiana	New Mexico
Pennsylvania	North Dakota	Oklahoma	California
Delaware	South Dakota	Texas	Oregon
Maryland	Nebraska	Kentucky	Washington
District of	Kansas	Tennessee	
Columbia 1/		Alabama	
		Mississippi	

1/ Includes also that part of the Washington, D.C., Standard Metropolitan
Area located in Virginia.

Identification of Respondents

The 106 FSU's of approximately 10,000 households were divided into segments.
A segment is a portion of an enumeration district in nontracted areas and is a
block (or blocks) in tracted areas. Seven hundred such segments were drawn.

A detailed map of the segments was given to each interviewer after proper instruction and she was asked to list each household in the segment. The lists were returned to the home office of the contractor where they were subsampled and a listing of the sampled households returned to the interviewers. The selection of segments and households within lists was made in such a way as to make the sample self-weighted.

The procedure of prelisting households and drawing the final sample in the office gave the contractor control over the selection of respondent households. Checks were made on the process of listing households.

An eligible household in this study was composed of the occupants of a dwelling unit in which a member of the household was responsible for purchase or care of household "linens." Every sample dwelling unit was contacted and every reasonable attempt was made to determine eligibility of the household and to interview the responsible household member. A differential callback rule based on zone and region was used. This yielded a completion rate of 75 percent of all eligible respondents.

A total of 3,835 prelisted dwelling units was visited to determine eligible households for eventual interviewing. Of this number, 446 were either vacant or no longer standing. Thus, 3,389 occupied households were designated as part of the survey sample. Of this number, 70 were households where no member had responsibility for purchase or care of sheets, blankets, and so on. The remaining 3,315 comprised the eligible group of sample households.

Interview completion rates among eligible respondents

Region and zone	Eligible households in survey sample	Completed interviews of eligible households	
	Number	Number	Percent
Region:			
Northeast.....:	986	713	72.3
North Central.:	951	735	77.3
South.........:	864	684	79.2
West..........:	518	357	68.9
Zone:			
City..........:	1,255	842	67.1
Suburb........:	980	750	76.5
Rural.........:	1,084	897	82.7
U.S. total.........:	3,319	2,489	75.0

28

Sampling Tolerances

Sampling tolerances were determined for the four following items: bed-
preads, tablecloths, rugs, and fabric. The computational method used for
nis determination was Hanson and Horwitz collapsed strata method for the
ncertainty PSU's, and the equation given for certainty PSU's.

Item	Coefficient of variation (V)	Ratio using (P)	Standard error of P (S_p)	Standard error of a random sample
edspreads	0.00484	0.959	0.00464	0.00397
ablecloths	.02003	.7404	.0148	.00879
ugs	.03270	.5034	.0165	.01000
abric	.02709	.4536	.0123	.00996

In the actual computation of the sampling errors, the errors for the
ertainty strata and the estimates of the noncertainty strata must be computed
y different methods. After these are both computed, they are added together.

To aid further in interpreting results, the following table is provided
o indicate the approximate magnitude of random error due to sampling:

Approximate sampling tolerances
(95 in 100 confidence level)

or percentages around --	Number of interviews on which a percentage is based					
	2,489*	2,000	1,000	750	500	200
	---------------------------Percent---------------------------					
50	3	3	4	4	5	8
40 or 60	3	3	4	4	5	8
30 or 70	2	3	4	4	5	7
20 or 80	2	3	3	3	4	6
10 or 90	2	2	2	3	3	5

* Size of total sample.

The chances are approximately 95 in 100 that the survey result does not vary, plus or minus, by more than the indicated amount from the result that would have been obtained had the same procedure been used to interview all homemakers in the population.

For example, 40 percent of all homemakers in the survey said that all cotton sheets keep their whiteness or color a long time. The chances are 95 in 100 that, had all homemakers in the population been interviewed, the true percentage of those saying this about all cotton sheets would be between 37 and 43 percent.

For subgroups of the sample, the possible variation is larger than for the total sample because the number of interviews was smaller. For instance, of the 509 respondents who had less than some high school education, 69 percent indicated that they had not used woven bedspreads. The chances are approximately 95 in 100 that if all homemakers with less than some high school education had been interviewed, between 64 and 74 percent would have been found not to use such bedspreads.

Explanation of Tables

Tables are presented in the order of questioning. Generally the wording used in the actual question, probes excluded, is the table heading. Tables are identified by the numbers of the questions on which they are based.

The tabulations are based on the total sample of 2,489 respondents, except where noted. Multiple answers were permitted on some questions. Although counted only once when answers are grouped into a summary category, a respondent may be counted in more than one subcategory within the summary category.

Questions 1, 4, 2, and 6: "...How long ago did you last get any sheets for use in your home -- excluding crib sheets or sheets for youth beds?" "...Any other in the past 12 months?" (Asked only if acquired any sheets in the 12 months prior to interviewing.) "Did you buy them or get them as a gift?"

	Cases	Acquired in past year				Between 1-3 years ago	More than 3 years ago	Don't know
		Bought only	Gift only	Both	Total			
	Number	Percent						
U.S. total	2489	37	5	4	46	34	19	
Community size:								
Metropolitan	846	41	3	5	49	30	19	2
Urban	746	37	5	3	46	37	16	2
Rural	897	33	6	5	44	34	21	1
Homemaker's education:								
8th grade or less	509	26	3	1	31	37	29	3
High school - 1-3 years	493	38	3	3	44	37	17	1
High school - 4 years	909	40	5	6	51	33	15	1
College - 1-3 years	346	46	6	6	58	28	14	1
College - over 3 years	220	37	7	7	51	32	15	1
Region:								
Northeast	713	39	5	3	47	30	20	2
North Central	735	37	3	4	45	35	19	1
South	684	38	5	4	48	35	16	1
West	357	33	6	6	45	34	20	1
Homemaker's age:								
Under 30	515	33	10	7	50	35	14	2
30 - 39	523	48	4	6	58	31	11	*
40 - 49	505	47	2	5	55	35	10	1
50 - 59	404	33	3	3	40	34	24	2
60 and over	538	24	4	1	29	34	35	3
Family income:								
Lower	822	26	5	2	34	36	27	3
Middle	731	39	5	5	50	34	16	1
Upper	722	47	4	6	57	32	11	1
Family size:								
1 or 2	1038	28	5	3	35	35	27	3
3 or 4	825	40	5	5	50	34	16	1
5 or more	626	50	5	6	61	30	9	*
Family composition:								
Adults only	1151	29	4	3	36	35	26	3
Children	1338	44	5	6	55	33	12	*

* Less than 1 percent

Questions 3 and 7: "How many did you get at that time?" (Asked only if acquired any sheets in the 12 months prior to interviewing.)

	Cases	Percent asked	One or two	Three or four	Five or six	Seven to twelve	More than twelve
	Number				Percent		
U.S. total	2489	46	11	14	10	9	2
Community size:							
Metropolitan	846	49	10	15	12	11	1
Urban	746	46	11	13	9	10	2
Rural	897	44	12	15	9	7	1
Homemaker's education:							
8th grade or less	509	31	8	11	6	5	1
High school - 1-3 years	493	44	10	15	11	7	2
High school - 4 years	909	51	12	16	11	10	2
College - 1-3 years	346	58	15	13	12	15	2
College - over 3 years	220	51	13	16	11	10	1
Region:							
Northeast	713	47	11	15	11	8	2
North Central	735	45	13	12	11	8	1
South	684	48	10	17	10	9	2
West	357	45	10	13	8	13	1
Homemaker's age:							
Under 30	515	50	12	15	10	10	2
30 - 39	523	58	12	17	15	12	2
40 - 49	505	55	10	16	12	14	2
50 - 59	404	40	12	11	8	7	2
60 and over	538	29	9	11	5	3	*
Family income:							
Lower	822	34	10	12	6	5	1
Middle	731	50	13	15	11	9	2
Upper	722	57	11	17	13	13	2

	Number	Percent						
U.S. total	2489	10	83	14	12	1	2	122
Community size:								
Metropolitan	846	12	78	18	15	1	2	126
Urban	746	9	79	16	12	1	3	120
Rural	897	8	89	9	9	1	1	118
Homemaker's education:								
8th grade or less	509	6	91	4	5	1	3	108
High school – 1-3 years	493	7	84	11	11	1	2	116
High school – 4 years	909	11	80	15	14	1	2	123
College – 1-3 years	346	13	75	25	17	1	2	134
College – over 3 years	220	14	80	25	14	4	2	137
Region:								
Northeast	713	10	81	14	11	1	3	120
North Central	735	11	80	16	13	1	2	123
South	684	9	87	11	10	1	1	119
West	357	10	81	17	15	1	2	126
Homemaker's age:								
Under 30	515	13	72	21	17	1	2	125
30 – 39	523	2	81	17	12	*	2	124
40 – 49	505	12	84	15	15	1	2	128
50 – 59	404	7	86	11	11	2	2	119
60 and over	538	5	90	7	5	1	3	111
Family income:								
Lower	822	6	88	6	8	1	2	110
Middle	731	11	81	14	11	1	3	121
Upper	722	14	79	23	17	2	1	136
Family size:								
1 or 2	1038	8	85	10	9	1	3	116
3 or 4	825	10	79	18	15	1	2	124
5 or more	626	12	84	16	12	1	1	126
Family composition:								
Adults only	1151	8	84	11	9	2	3	117
Children	1338	11	81	17	14	1	2	126

* Less than 1 percent

33

	Polyester and cotton blend	All cotton	Durable press-polyester and cotton	Durable press-all cotton
			Percent	
1- Not a very good choice for me	12	11	10	8
2-	9	9	6	7
3-	25	16	16	15
4-	22	17	18	23
5- A very good choice for me	27	47	45	42
Mean	3.47	3.81	3.86	3.89
Did not rate	7	*	5	5
Number of cases	2489	2489	2489	2489

Question 11: "...Which of these ideas would be most important to you if you were buying sheets?"

	U.S. total
	Percent
Lasts a long time	63
Easy to wash	57
Looks good without ironing	55
Good value for the money	55
Keeps its whiteness or color	48
Can be bleached	33
Easy to remove stains	31
Smooth to the touch	29
Can buy it on sale	28
Easy to dry	27
A certain fiber, such as cotton...	18
A weave, such as muslin or percale	17
Good range of colors and prints	16
Does not "pill"	13
Absorbent	5
Total	496
Number of cases	2489

Question 12: "...Which of these phrases describe your opinions about polyester and cotton blend sheets? Any others?"

	Number of cases	Easy to wash	Not easy to wash	Looks good without ironing	Does not look good without ironing	Smooth to the touch	Rough to the touch	Easy to remove stains	Difficult to remove stains	Can be bleached	Must not be bleached	Keeps its whiteness	Does not keep its whiteness	Lasts a long time	Wears out rather quickly	Good value for the money	Not good value for the money	Absorbent	Not absorbent	Can buy it on sale	Cannot buy it on sale	Does not 'pill'	'Pills'	Easy to dry	Not easy to dry	Good range of colors	Not a good range of colors	None of these	Don't know, no answer	Total
														–Percent–																
U.S. total	2489	50	1	46	7	31	1	15	9	16	16	21	9	34	5	21	4	7	7	19	3	11	5	42	1	21	1	*	23	418
Community size:																														
Metropolitan	846	49	1	44	9	33	1	15	10	16	16	22	10	30	6	22	5	8	10	24	3	14	5	41	1	27	1	1	24	448
Urban	746	54	1	47	6	31	1	15	10	10	18	21	10	35	6	20	4	7	7	20	2	10	4	44	1	17	1	1	19	419
Rural	897	50	1	45	5	30	*	14	7	14	14	20	7	36	3	19	2	6	6	14	3	8	4	42	1	19	1	1	24	391
Homemaker's education:																														
8th grade or less	69	39	1	35	5	21	1	12	6	6	11	16	6	24	4	16	3	5	4	15	3	9	3	31	1	15	*	*	39	337
High school – 1-3 years	93	49	2	47	5	28	1	17	9	11	16	22	8	36	5	20	4	8	5	18	2	11	5	44	1	19	1	1	20	414
High school – 4 years	99	55	1	49	7	33	2	16	10	13	18	23	10	37	5	21	4	5	8	21	2	14	5	46	1	22	1	1	17	444
College – 1-3 years	86	55	1	50	8	40	1	14	10	16	21	20	10	36	6	26	4	7	10	14	4	15	5	45	1	25	1	1	18	457
College – over 3 years	20	53	1	44	10	40	2	14	12	11	20	20	10	36	5	21	4	5	10	19	5	7	7	46	1	29	1	*	20	456
Region:																														
Northeast	713	51	1	42	7	29	1	14	7	16	16	18	8	29	4	16	3	6	5	19	3	10	4	39	1	20	*	*	23	385
North Central	735	51	1	50	7	33	1	17	11	18	18	25	11	36	6	26	4	9	10	22	3	14	5	47	*	24	1	1	21	466
South	684	54	1	42	6	27	2	16	8	13	16	18	5	32	4	18	4	6	6	14	2	8	5	38	1	16	1	1	25	369
West	357	53	1	49	7	40	2	16	12	16	20	25	11	41	6	23	6	6	11	23	6	16	7	47	1	26	2	2	20	482
Homemaker's age:																														
Under 30	515	53	2	43	9	34	1	16	11	16	18	23	10	37	4	24	3	8	8	22	2	14	5	44	1	27	1	1	18	454
30 – 39	523	51	1	51	6	34	1	16	11	16	16	19	9	37	6	21	4	6	7	20	4	10	6	48	1	22	2	1	16	435
40 – 49	505	54	1	50	8	31	1	16	10	16	16	21	9	33	4	22	5	7	6	21	4	8	6	47	1	21	1	1	20	450
50 – 59	404	52	1	50	5	31	1	9	7	12	15	21	6	27	3	20	4	7	5	16	3	11	5	41	1	20	1	1	23	421
60 and over	538	39	*	35	5	23	1	6	8	11	12	20	6	27	3	17	2	6	5	16	8	8	4	31	1	15	1	1	36	338
Family income:																														
Lower	822	43	1	39	6	24	1	12	10	14	15	18	5	30	5	16	3	6	4	18	3	9	3	35	1	17	*	*	31	356
Middle	731	55	1	48	7	34	1	17	12	16	18	24	10	37	6	23	5	7	7	18	3	11	7	48	1	22	1	*	18	453
Upper	722	54	1	52	8	38	2	16	12	17	18	23	12	37	5	25	3	8	10	23	4	14	5	48	1	25	1	1	16	473
Family size:																														
1 or 2	1038	45	1	42	6	28	1	13	9	13	17	21	7	31	4	18	3	6	6	18	2	10	5	36	1	18	1	1	30	380
3 or 4	825	55	1	47	8	33	1	16	13	16	18	22	11	36	5	23	4	8	7	23	3	11	6	44	1	23	1	1	18	442
5 or more	626	50	2	49	7	33	1	17	13	16	20	25	10	36	6	23	4	6	9	22	4	11	6	50	*	23	1	*	18	450
Family composition:																														
Adults only	1151	46	1	42	6	28	1	13	10	14	18	18	8	31	4	18	3	6	6	18	3	8	6	37	1	18	1	1	28	383
Children	1338	53	1	49	7	34	1	17	13	17	18	22	10	36	6	22	4	7	8	20	2	12	7	47	1	23	1	1	18	449

* Less than 1 percent

36

Question 13: "Which of these describe your opinions about all cotton sheets? Any others?"

—Percent—

	Cases	Easy to wash	Not easy to wash	Looks good without ironing	Does not look good without ironing	Smooth to the touch	Rough to the touch	Easy to remove stains	Difficult to remove stains	Can be bleached	Must not be bleached	Keeps its whiteness	Does not keep its whiteness	Whitens	L, a long time	Wears out rather quickly	Good value for the money	Not good value for the money	Absorbent	Not absorbent	Can buy it on sale	Cannot buy it on sale	Does not 'pill'	'Pills'	Easy to dry	Not easy to dry	Good range of colors	Not a good range of colors	None of these	Don't know, no answer	Total
U.S. total	2489	63	2	14	38	21	14	38	7	64	1	40	1	6	60	6	43	2	23	1	47	*	19	3	28	2	28	2	*	2	582
Community size:																															
Metropolitan	846	63	2	18	44	25	16	35	8	62	1	41	1	8	59	8	42	2	27	2	48	*	21	5	29	2	32	3	-	2	607
Urban	746	59	2	16	36	18	15	37	7	63	1	39	1	6	58	6	43	3	23	1	45	1	2	4	28	14	23	1	1	1	566
Rural	897	67	3	14	33	20	11	41	6	66	1	40	*	4	61	4	44	2	20	1	47	*	18	1	26	10	28	1	*	3	572
Homemaker's education:																															
8th grade or less	509	70	2	18	29	25	9	42	4	65	1	43	1	5	62	5	47	2	22	2	48	1	18	3	33	8	26	1	1	3	591
High school – 1-3 years	493	63	3	15	35	21	2	38	5	64	1	41	1	5	56	5	47	3	21	1	45	2	2	3	27	11	25	2	1	3	569
High school – 4 years	909	62	2	14	39	19	16	37	8	64	1	39	1	8	60	8	42	3	23	1	48	1	19	4	27	11	27	1	1	1	572
College – 1-3 years	346	61	3	11	47	21	13	33	10	62	1	39	1	9	53	9	40	3	27	1	46	-	22	4	24	22	32	3	*	2	592
College – over 3 years	220	60	1	7	47	20	7	41	4	59	2	39	2	7	52	7	41	3	27	1	45	-	16	5	22	16	39	3	*	2	593
Region:																															
Northeast	713	65	1	17	39	24	13	32	5	61	1	41	1	5	59	5	40	2	22	1	44	*	18	2	27	10	26	1	*	2	560
North Central	735	60	4	15	43	21	18	36	9	64	1	41	1	9	58	9	48	1	26	1	46	*	23	4	32	13	29	1	*	1	616
South	684	67	2	16	27	19	2	38	4	67	*	40	*	3	62	3	41	3	18	1	48	1	11	3	23	10	26	1	-	1	549
West	357	62	1	11	45	20	20	38	9	62	1	39	1	11	58	11	41	2	29	1	50	-	26	4	30	16	35	3	-	2	624
Homemaker's age:																															
Under 30	515	62	3	15	43	21	15	33	10	58	1	35	1	9	55	9	39	2	23	1	47	*	19	5	32	11	31	3	*	3	581
30 – 39	523	61	1	15	39	16	16	38	8	64	1	35	1	7	57	7	39	3	22	1	45	2	2	5	23	14	28	1	*	2	563
40 – 49	505	63	3	13	41	19	13	41	7	64	1	39	1	6	59	6	40	2	25	1	48	1	18	4	27	13	28	1	*	2	589
50 – 59	404	65	2	14	33	24	13	41	4	69	1	44	1	4	64	4	47	1	22	*	44	1	20	2	30	11	27	1	*	2	593
60 and over	538	66	3	15	33	25	10	39	4	65	*	47	*	4	63	4	50	1	22	*	46	*	20	2	28	10	26	1	*	2	589
Family income:																															
Lower	822	68	2	16	30	23	10	39	5	65	1	43	1	6	63	6	46	1	22	1	46	*	19	2	31	10	26	2	*	2	581
Middle	731	64	3	15	39	20	14	38	8	65	1	41	1	6	58	6	41	3	22	1	48	*	18	3	30	11	28	1	*	2	583
Upper	722	57	2	11	47	18	20	37	8	62	1	38	1	8	58	8	41	3	27	1	42	*	20	4	23	30	30	3	1	1	590
Family size:																															
1 or 2	1038	62	3	13	35	23	13	37	6	62	1	42	1	6	61	6	45	1	22	1	44	*	19	2	27	10	26	2	*	2	570
3 or 4	825	66	2	13	40	20	14	39	7	64	1	38	1	7	59	7	40	2	25	1	48	*	20	3	28	13	29	2	1	1	590
5 or more	626	62	2	15	39	19	17	38	8	67	*	39	*	5	58	5	43	2	24	2	50	*	18	3	28	13	30	2	*	1	593
Family composition:																															
Adults only	1151	62	3	13	35	23	12	37	6	61	1	42	1	6	61	6	44	2	22	1	43	1	18	2	27	11	26	2	*	2	567
Children	1338	65	2	14	40	20	16	39	8	66	1	38	1	6	58	6	42	2	24	1	50	*	19	4	28	2	30	2	1	1	595

* Less than 1 percent

37

Question 14: "Which of these describe your opinions about durable or permanent press sheets made of polyester and cotton blend? Any others?"

-Percent

	Cases (Number)	Easy to wash	Not easy to wash	Looks good without ironing	Does not look good without ironing	Smooth to the touch	Rough to the touch	Easy to remove stains	Difficult to remove stains	Can be bleached	Must not be bleached	Keeps its whiteness	Does not keep its whiteness	Lasts a long time	Wears out rather quickly	Good value for the money	Not good value for the money	Absorbent	Not absorbent	Can buy it on sale	Cannot buy it on sale	Does not 'pill'	'Pills'	Easy to dry	Not easy to dry	Good range of colors	Not a good range of colors	None of these	Don't know, no answer	Total
U.S. total	2489	46	1	60	2	37	1	12	11	8	18	17	8	27	20	6	4	6	9	17	4	11	4	43	1	22	1	1	24	419
Community size:																														
Metropolitan	846	45	2	59	2	39	1	13	12	9	18	18	9	27	20	5	4	6	11	21	4	13	4	43	1	27	1	*	25	439
Urban	746	47	1	64	2	39	1	13	11	8	18	18	7	27	20	5	4	7	11	18	5	11	4	45	1	18	1	1	20	425
Rural	897	45	1	57	3	32	1	10	10	6	16	16	7	28	19	3	3	6	7	12	4	9	5	43	1	19	1	1	27	396
Homemaker's education:																														
8th grade or less	509	31	2	42	2	23	1	9	7	6	15	11	6	18	13	2	4	5	12	12	5	8	2	31	1	14	1	4	44	320
High school – 1-3 years	493	44	3	60	3	38	1	14	10	7	19	16	8	29	21	4	4	7	18	18	5	12	5	47	2	20	1	*	23	429
High school – 4 years	909	52	1	65	1	42	1	12	11	8	20	16	7	31	21	4	4	6	10	20	5	12	5	48	1	28	2	1	17	451
College – 1-3 years	346	52	1	67	2	42	1	14	10	10	16	22	8	29	23	5	5	7	18	20	5	12	5	46	1	28	1	*	18	456
College – over 3 years	220	48	2	64	2	42	1	12	15	10	16	17	11	25	19	4	4	8	13	18	6	13	4	46	1	28	2	*	22	446
Region:																														
Northeast	713	49	1	56	2	37	1	12	9	9	16	16	9	27	17	2	4	9	17	15	7	9	3	42	1	20	1	1	24	395
North Central	735	47	1	64	2	42	1	13	11	8	21	16	9	30	24	5	5	7	11	17	3	10	5	46	*	21	1	1	21	471
South	684	39	1	58	2	29	1	10	11	4	18	11	7	23	16	5	3	6	13	13	8	8	5	38	1	18	1	1	29	365
West	357	50	1	61	2	39	1	15	11	11	14	24	8	32	22	6	6	5	11	21	3	13	5	50	1	26	1	–	23	466
Homemaker's age:																														
Under 30	515	53	2	68	1	43	1	17	14	11	21	23	6	32	26	3	4	9	10	21	3	14	4	50	1	30	1	1	16	491
30 – 39	523	49	1	66	2	40	1	17	11	11	18	16	7	30	20	4	5	6	11	17	5	11	4	49	1	25	1	1	16	446
40 – 49	505	50	1	65	2	38	1	12	11	9	19	18	10	31	20	5	5	6	11	17	5	11	4	48	*	21	1	1	21	445
50 – 59	404	46	1	58	1	37	1	12	10	6	19	19	7	25	17	5	5	5	9	18	3	10	4	44	1	19	1	1	26	409
60 and over	538	32	1	41	3	25	1	8	6	6	12	11	5	19	14	3	3	5	4	11	8	8	3	28	1	13	1	1	42	308
Family income:																														
Lower	822	38	1	49	2	31	1	11	11	5	16	13	6	23	15	3	4	5	15	15	3	9	3	35	1	16	1	1	34	353
Middle	731	52	1	63	2	40	1	13	13	9	21	16	8	29	21	4	5	10	16	16	5	10	4	47	1	23	1	1	18	449
Upper	722	51	1	70	2	43	1	12	14	9	19	24	9	30	24	5	5	6	13	22	5	15	5	52	1	28	1	*	17	485
Family size:																														
1 or 2	1038	39	1	50	2	31	1	10	7	6	14	14	6	23	16	3	3	5	6	15	3	9	4	35	1	18	1	1	34	355
3 or 4	825	50	1	69	3	41	1	15	12	9	21	20	8	31	22	4	5	8	10	17	4	14	5	49	1	25	1	*	18	469
5 or more	626	51	1	64	1	41	1	10	13	8	19	19	10	30	20	5	5	6	12	19	8	11	7	50	1	25	1	*	18	461
Family composition:																														
Adults only	1151	40	1	51	3	31	1	11	8	7	14	14	6	23	16	4	3	5	6	15	3	9	3	35	1	18	1	1	32	360
Children	1338	51	1	67	2	41	1	14	13	9	21	20	9	31	23	4	4	7	11	19	5	13	6	50	1	25	1	*	18	470

* Less than 1 percent

Question 15: "Which of these describe your opinions about durable or permanent press sheets made of all cotton? Any others?"

	Number of cases	Easy to wash	Not easy to wash	Looks good without ironing	Does not look good without ironing	Smooth to the touch	Rough to the touch	Easy to remove stains	Difficult to remove stains	Can be bleached	Must not be bleached	Keeps its whiteness	Does not keep its whiteness	Lasts a long time	Wears out rather quickly	Good value for the money	Not good value for the money	Absorbent	Not absorbent	Can buy it on sale	Cannot buy it on sale	Does not 'pill'	'Pills'	Easy to dry	Not easy to dry	Good range of colors	Not a good range of colors	None of these	Don't know, no answer	Total
															--Percent--															
U.S. total	2489	47	1	54	5	31	3	16	8	17	10	21	5	32	23	23	3	11	6	19	4	12	3	39	22	22	*	1	24	83
Community size:																														
Metropolitan	846	47	2	51	6	32	3	16	8	19	10	23	5	31	24	24	3	11	7	22	4	16	2	38	28	28	*	1	26	41
Urban	746	46	*	58	5	32	3	15	7	19	11	22	5	39	22	22	3	10	5	20	1	11	3	39	18	18	1	1	21	49
Rural	897	49	1	54	4	30	3	15	8	15	8	17	5	40	23	23	3	10	5	16	4	10	4	40	21	21	1	1	25	09
Homemaker's education:																														
8th grade or less	69	39	1	46	5	23	3	14	4	17	9	15	4	31	17	17	2	8	4	15	4	9	2	31	16	16	1	*	37	52
High school – 1-3 years	93	47	1	55	5	32	3	15	7	12	11	20	5	39	26	26	2	11	6	21	5	20	2	39	23	23	*	1	23	88
High school – 4 years	99	51	1	58	6	33	3	15	9	19	12	23	5	44	24	24	4	11	6	19	4	14	3	44	24	24	1	1	19	60
College – 1-3 years	96	51	1	56	5	36	4	16	10	20	10	23	6	39	22	22	4	9	8	21	2	13	3	39	26	26	1	1	20	87
College – over 3 years	20	50	2	54	6	36	4	16	10	17	7	21	5	41	25	25	2	11	8	21	1	13	3	41	26	26	1	1	25	49
Region:																														
Northeast	713	49	1	51	7	31	4	14	5	16	9	19	4	38	20	20	2	9	4	18	4	10	1	38	19	19	*	*	23	92
North Central	735	48	1	53	5	33	3	19	8	18	11	25	5	42	26	26	4	14	7	23	5	17	2	42	24	24	1	1	24	65
South	684	50	1	59	5	29	3	12	9	20	10	17	5	41	22	22	4	7	7	16	4	16	3	41	20	20	1	1	25	90
West	357	46	3	55	6	31	3	18	10	15	8	23	5	41	24	24	4	11	9	21	6	16	3	41	27	27	*	*	24	60
Homemaker's age:																														
Under 30	515	51	2	58	4	34	2	17	12	15	5	23	3	42	28	28	3	11	6	22	3	13	2	42	27	27	1	1	18	62
30 – 39	523	53	1	57	6	32	2	15	7	18	6	20	5	45	24	24	4	10	6	21	5	13	2	45	25	25	*	*	18	88
40 – 49	505	51	1	59	5	32	2	15	9	20	11	21	6	43	24	24	2	13	7	23	3	14	3	43	22	22	*	*	22	69
50 – 59	404	47	1	55	7	34	3	15	8	20	10	21	5	41	23	23	3	11	7	21	5	12	2	41	23	23	*	*	23	87
60 and over	538	35	1	44	4	24	3	12	4	17	7	24	3	27	17	17	2	9	3	21	4	11	1	27	14	14	1	1	38	35
Family income:																														
Lower	822	42	1	50	3	26	4	14	6	13	10	17	4	33	18	18	2	8	4	17	4	10	2	33	18	18	1	1	31	369
Middle	731	42	1	57	7	34	2	15	7	18	12	25	5	43	26	26	4	11	7	25	5	13	4	43	23	23	1	1	19	448
Upper	722	50	2	58	6	36	3	18	9	16	9	17	5	43	27	27	3	13	8	25	3	16	3	43	27	27	1	1	19	475
Family size:																														
1 or 2	1038	40	1	49	5	27	3	13	5	15	7	18	3	33	20	20	3	10	4	17	3	10	2	33	18	18	1	1	32	371
3 or 4	825	52	1	59	6	35	3	19	8	18	10	24	6	43	26	26	4	12	6	21	5	15	2	43	26	26	*	*	18	462
5 or more	626	54	1	58	5	33	3	15	10	20	12	21	5	45	25	25	3	9	8	21	5	12	4	45	24	24	*	*	20	457
Family composition:																														
Adults only	1151	41	1	49	5	27	3	13	6	15	7	18	4	33	19	19	2	9	4	17	3	11	2	33	18	18	1	1	31	372
Children	1338	53	1	59	5	34	3	18	9	19	12	23	6	45	26	26	3	12	7	22	4	14	3	45	26	26	1	*	18	466

* Less than 1 percent

Question 16: "How do you usually care for your sheets?"

	Cases	Wash and dry - commercial laundry	Machine wash - home or laundermat	Machine dry - home or laundermat	Dry on clothesline	Dry line or machine - depending on weather	Other	Total
	Number-------------------------Percent-----------------------------							
U.S. total	2489	7	87	28	37	25	2	186
Community size:								
Metropolitan	846	11	85	38	28	18	3	183
Urban	746	8	87	26	39	26	1	188
Rural	897	4	88	21	42	32	1	188
Homemaker's education:								
8th grade or less	509	5	86	20	53	18	3	185
High school - 1-3 years	493	6	88	24	39	29	1	188
High school - 4 years	909	6	90	30	33	29	1	188
College - 1-3 years	346	11	84	32	29	25	2	183
College - over 3 years	220	15	80	41	19	24	3	183
Region:								
Northeast	713	10	85	24	38	23	3	182
North Central	735	7	88	30	28	33	*	186
South	684	6	86	24	48	21	2	187
West	357	7	91	41	29	25	1	193
Homemaker's age:								
Under 30	515	7	88	37	26	28	1	187
30 - 39	523	5	92	31	29	31	1	189
40 - 49	505	5	89	29	38	27	1	189
50 - 59	404	9	86	24	42	24	1	186
60 and over	538	12	80	19	49	17	3	181
Family income:								
Lower	822	7	85	21	47	21	3	183
Middle	731	7	89	28	35	29	1	188
Upper	722	8	88	38	25	28	1	188
Family size:								
1 or 2	1038	12	81	27	38	19	2	180
3 or 4	825	4	90	29	36	29	2	190
5 or more	626	3	92	28	35	31	1	191
Family composition:								
Adults only	1151	12	82	27	39	20	2	182
Children	1338	4	91	29	34	30	1	190

* Less than 1 percent

40

Question 17: "...As I mention different kinds of blankets, tell me how good a choice for you each blanket would be if you were buying blankets now..."

	All wool	All cotton	All synthetic	Regular	Electric	Thermal
			Percent			
1- Not a very good choice for me	43	23	17	10	43	21
2-	10	15	9	8	8	7
3-	13	21	21	22	11	14
4-	9	15	22	22	9	19
5- A very good choice for me	25	24	27	36	27	35
Mean	2.64	3.02	3.34	3.67	2.68	3.40
Did not rate	1	*	4	2	1	4
Number of cases	2489	2489	2489	2489	2489	2489

* Less than 1 percent

41

Question 18: "...Which of these ideas would be most important if you were
buying blankets? Any others?"

	U.S. total
	Percent
Can be washed	84
Does not shrink	68
Lasts a long time	60
Good value for the money	50
Colors stay like new	43
Good for use all year round	39
Does not stretch	37
Does not 'pill'	34
A certain fiber, such as cotton...	28
Easy to remove stains	26
Does not burn easily -- not flammable	22
Can buy it on sale	21
Good range of colors	20
Total	531
Number of cases	2489

Question 19: "...Which of these describe your opinions about all wool blankets? Any others?"

	Cases (Number)	Can be washed	Must not be washed	Easy to remove stains	Difficult to remove stains	Colors stay like new	Colors do not stay like new	Lasts a long time	Wears out rather quickly	Good value for the money	Not good value for the money	Can buy it on sale	Cannot buy it on sale	Does not 'pill'	'Pills'	Good range of colors	Not a good range of colors	Shrinks	Does not shrink	Stretches	Does not stretch	Does not burn easily -- not flammable	Burns easily -- flammable	Good for use all year round	Not good for use all year round	None of these	Don't know, no answer	Total
													-Percent-															
U. S. total	2489	26	44	7	27	33	5	58	2	32	7	20	4	13	22	28	2	52	11	7	19	10	13	9	45	1	4	503
Community size:																												
Metropolitan	846	28	42	10	25	37	7	64	3	37	5	25	4	16	22	34	2	46	13	7	21	10	14	13	40	1	5	528
Urban	746	25	46	5	30	31	6	54	3	32	8	22	3	11	26	26	2	56	2	8	19	10	2	7	52	1	4	512
Rural	897	26	45	6	26	31	4	55	1	28	9	14	6	12	19	24	2	56	10	5	16	8	2	6	43	1	4	472
Homemaker's education:																												
8th grade or less	509	30	37	10	20	32	5	56	3	33	7	24	5	16	25	25	2	44	14	6	22	10	11	9	39	1	7	480
High school – 1-3 years	493	24	48	5	31	30	5	52	3	32	9	19	4	11	22	26	2	56	2	7	18	8	13	6	45	1	4	493
High school – 4 years	909	26	47	8	28	31	6	55	3	30	6	23	3	11	24	27	2	58	2	5	16	11	13	8	47	2	4	497
College – 1-3 years	346	27	44	7	27	40	5	67	3	38	8	21	2	15	24	35	2	48	10	5	22	11	13	11	47	1	4	542
College – over 3 years	220	27	45	7	26	36	5	67	1	44	5	22	5	15	29	35	3	45	13	5	20	14	11	15	43	1	4	544
Region:																												
Northeast	713	31	39	8	23	30	6	61	3	34	5	22	2	15	23	31	2	47	2	7	14	8	9	11	45	1	6	490
North Central	735	27	45	5	31	35	5	53	3	33	9	19	2	11	26	20	3	59	11	4	18	9	2	8	48	1	5	534
South	684	20	48	4	27	36	4	53	1	38	7	14	4	11	17	31	3	46	11	6	24	10	11	4	43	2	2	449
West	357	26	46	8	26	38	6	67	2	41	9	26	6	18	24	33	5	60	13	6	24	13	14	17	41	1	2	573
Homemaker's age:																												
Under 30	515	18	49	5	29	27	9	59	3	28	9	18	4	17	27	25	6	52	10	8	16	10	14	9	46	1	6	496
30 - 39	523	24	46	7	29	30	5	55	2	27	7	17	6	11	24	29	2	54	14	7	14	8	11	7	50	2	3	488
40 - 49	505	25	49	8	28	36	5	56	2	27	8	21	2	14	21	29	2	56	13	5	20	10	15	10	45	1	3	520
50 - 59	404	28	44	7	28	39	6	60	3	35	7	25	3	14	25	30	1	54	14	7	20	10	15	10	41	1	6	495
60 and over	538	37	34	9	20	35	4	59	2	44	6	22	3	16	14	29	1	45	14	5	22	10	11	10	41	1	6	495
Family income:																												
Lower	822	30	40	8	23	30	6	57	3	31	8	20	4	13	18	28	2	47	13	6	19	10	2	9	42	1	6	485
Middle	731	24	44	7	30	33	5	57	3	33	7	19	3	11	24	28	3	55	11	6	19	10	13	9	47	1	4	508
Upper	722	23	50	5	30	34	6	60	2	33	7	23	3	14	28	30	2	57	9	8	18	9	13	9	48	1	3	528
Family size:																												
1 or 2	1038	31	39	7	22	34	6	58	2	35	7	21	4	13	18	28	2	48	12	5	21	10	12	10	41	1	5	495
3 or 4	825	25	46	9	28	33	7	57	3	31	7	20	3	14	24	29	2	53	12	9	17	9	14	9	44	1	4	511
5 or more	626	22	51	7	32	31	5	58	2	29	8	19	5	12	25	26	3	57	10	5	17	9	11	7	52	1	4	508
Family composition:																												
Adults only	1151	31	38	7	23	35	5	58	2	36	6	21	4	14	19	28	2	48	12	5	21	9	12	11	40	1	5	496
Children	1338	22	49	7	30	32	6	57	2	29	8	19	4	13	25	28	3	56	11	8	17	10	13	8	49	1	4	510

* Less than 1 percent

Question 20: "Which of these describe your opinions about all cotton blankets? Any others?"

	Cases (Number)	Can be washed	Must not be washed	Easy to remove stains	Difficult to remove stains	Colors stay like new	Colors do not stay like new	Lasts a long time	Wears out rather quickly	Good value for the money	Not good value for the money	Can buy it on sale	Cannot buy it on sale	Does not 'pill'	'Pills'	Good range of colors	Not a good range of colors	Shrinks	Does not shrink	Stretches	Does not stretch	Does not burn easily -- not flammable	Burns easily -- flammable	Good for use all year round	Not good for use all year round	None of these	Don't know, no answer	Total
	Number													Percent														
U. S. total	2489	85	*	37	3	25	13	34	19	33	7	39	1	14	16	31	2	14	37	9	23	9	9	46	12	*	5	523
Community size:																												
Metropolitan	846	82	1	34	5	20	18	27	25	27	9	37	1	16	17	31	2	14	31	11	20	10	12	38	18	*	8	513
Urban	746	84	1	36	4	27	10	38	17	35	5	38	1	19	19	31	1	15	41	10	26	7	8	46	12	*	5	532
Rural	897	88	-	40	2	27	12	37	15	35	6	41	1	13	13	32	2	13	39	7	22	7	8	54	6	1	3	527
Homemaker's education:																												
8th grade or less	509	83	1	40	2	30	10	42	15	38	6	41	2	16	13	32	2	11	38	9	26	12	8	46	9	*	5	538
High school - 1-3 years	493	86	*	36	3	26	11	37	18	37	7	41	*	14	16	31	2	15	42	8	24	10	8	45	11	*	3	532
High school - 4 years	909	86	*	36	3	24	13	33	19	30	5	39	1	12	17	34	1	13	38	11	23	8	12	47	11	1	4	515
College - 1-3 years	346	85	1	38	5	20	20	26	24	31	9	38	1	14	20	34	3	16	11	9	23	7	12	41	15	1	8	528
College - over 3 years	220	80	1	34	4	16	18	25	24	25	12	32	1	13	16	27	2	16	28	7	18	9	12	50	15	-	8	499
Region:																												
Northeast	713	86	*	32	3	23	14	30	20	25	7	33	1	16	12	28	2	11	38	7	22	9	5	40	18	*	5	486
N rth Central	735	84	1	39	4	30	14	37	20	36	6	42	1	17	18	36	2	15	41	8	25	8	14	53	9	*	6	570
South	684	86	1	39	3	25	8	35	20	31	4	38	1	18	13	28	1	13	33	8	20	7	6	46	7	1	4	497
West	357	83	1	36	4	17	23	24	30	28	13	40	1	10	26	35	3	19	34	13	25	10	14	44	14	1	6	552
Homemaker's age:																												
Under 30	515	85	-	37	5	23	16	33	20	31	8	42	1	15	18	34	2	13	37	9	23	10	12	45	11	-	6	533
30 - 39	523	87	1	36	3	19	16	31	21	28	8	37	1	16	16	31	2	15	33	11	18	6	11	45	13	1	4	502
40 - 49	505	86	*	37	3	27	12	35	20	35	6	38	1	13	17	29	2	11	41	12	29	9	11	50	11	*	5	535
50 - 59	404	84	*	38	3	20	13	36	19	35	6	43	1	16	13	33	2	15	39	10	24	10	10	43	12	1	5	545
60 and over	538	83	1	36	3	26	10	34	17	35	5	36	1	15	13	30	2	14	36	6	26	11	6	46	13	1	6	509
Family income:																												
Lower	822	87	*	37	3	27	13	39	17	36	5	41	1	15	14	32	1	13	37	8	25	10	9	46	12	*	4	532
Middle	731	85	1	39	3	22	14	31	20	31	8	38	1	18	18	31	2	15	35	10	21	9	9	45	13	*	4	517
Upper	722	85	1	36	4	26	15	30	24	35	8	40	1	16	17	31	3	14	39	8	21	8	11	49	12	1	6	541
Family size:																												
1 or 2	1038	83	1	34	3	26	11	33	18	34	6	37	1	13	13	31	2	13	36	7	23	10	9	43	12	*	6	507
3 or 4	825	86	*	38	4	24	15	33	20	31	7	41	*	14	14	31	2	16	35	11	21	9	9	48	13	*	5	530
5 or more	626	87	*	39	4	23	16	36	20	32	7	40	1	15	15	31	2	13	41	10	24	7	11	49	11	*	4	542
Family composition:																												
Adults only	1151	82	1	33	3	25	12	32	18	33	6	36	1	13	15	31	2	13	36	7	23	10	9	42	12	1	6	504
Children	1338	87	*	39	4	24	15	35	20	33	7	41	1	14	17	32	2	15	38	11	22	8	10	49	12	*	4	540

* Less than 1 percent

44

Question 21: "Which of these describe your opinions about blankets made of an all synthetic fiber? Any others?"

	Cases (Number)	Can be washed	Must not be washed	Easy to remove stains	Difficult to remove stains	Colors stay like new	Colors do not stay like new	Lasts a long time	Wears out rather quickly	Good value for the money	Not good value for the money	Can buy it on sale	Cannot buy it on sale	Does not 'pill'	'Pills'	Good range of colors	Not a good range of colors	Shrinks	Does not shrink	Stretches	Does not stretch	Does not burn easily -- not flammable	Burns easily -- flammable	Good for use all year round	Not good for use all year round	None of these	Don't know, no answer	Total
														Percent														
U. S. total	2489	61	3	16	10	36	3	34	6	30	4	26	1	12	17	35	1	6	33	7	22	9	11	38	5	*	20	446
Community size:																												
Metropolitan	846	64	4	17	11	33	3	30	8	28	5	29	2	13	18	37	1	8	31	8	21	7	13	39	6	*	18	454
Urban	746	60	3	11	10	40	2	37	5	32	3	27	1	13	18	34	1	6	37	6	21	9	10	36	6	*	22	459
Rural	897	58	3	15	10	29	4	35	5	28	3	21	1	11	14	35	1	5	31	6	20	9	9	39	4	*	21	428
Homemaker's education:																												
8th grade or less	509	44	6	11	6	26	3	27	5	20	4	18	2	9	10	25	*	3	23	3	17	7	2	27	5	1	39	348
High school - 1-3 years	493	56	6	17	10	37	2	32	7	33	5	27	1	16	16	36	1	8	32	8	21	10	10	35	6	1	19	449
High school - 4 years	909	67	3	21	10	40	3	37	5	31	5	31	1	13	23	43	1	8	41	8	24	8	15	41	4	*	16	462
College - 1-3 years	346	71	3	18	8	34	2	44	4	35	5	31	*	15	21	42	1	8	44	4	24	8	13	45	2	1	12	525
College - over 3 years	220	70	3	18	8	33	4	36	10	32	3	27	*	13	21	42	1	4	34	2	25	2	13	47	6	2	12	490
Region:																												
Northeast	713	61	3	16	7	27	4	27	6	24	3	25	1	9	20	31	*	5	31	2	19	7	15	36	4	*	21	403
N rth Central	735	64	5	20	11	42	3	37	9	33	3	30	1	16	11	29	1	9	39	9	25	8	2	42	5	*	19	500
South	684	51	5	11	13	34	2	33	3	28	3	19	1	10	22	45	1	4	26	4	18	10	14	30	2	1	25	384
West	357	72	3	20	13	48	3	43	7	38	6	31	1	14	22	39	*	10	40	8	28	11	14	51	4	3	13	542
Homemaker's age:																												
Under 30	515	63	6	13	13	39	3	36	8	32	4	27	1	14	22	39	*	9	30	9	22	8	15	41	6	*	11	476
30 - 39	523	72	2	20	13	40	4	37	8	33	3	29	1	11	18	35	1	8	43	6	26	8	2	42	6	1	11	492
40 - 49	505	66	3	18	9	37	3	38	6	33	3	27	1	13	17	36	1	10	32	7	24	10	10	42	5	*	10	471
50 - 59	404	57	4	16	10	37	3	35	5	29	3	27	*	13	9	27	*	6	21	4	21	10	10	36	6	1	25	445
60 and over	538	45	4	11	6	28	3	36	2	22	4	20	1	9	9	31	1	4	25	4	16	6	7	29	4	1	37	352
Family income:																												
Lower	822	48	5	12	7	31	2	29	6	24	4	22	2	9	11	29	1	5	26	5	16	8	8	32	4	*	31	374
Middle	731	64	3	19	12	38	4	37	7	33	4	26	1	13	20	36	1	7	35	8	22	10	13	41	7	*	15	476
Upper	722	74	2	18	13	43	3	38	7	36	4	31	1	15	21	42	1	6	41	8	28	8	13	46	5	*	11	517
Family size:																												
1 or 2	1038	51	4	13	8	31	3	29	5	26	3	23	1	11	13	31	*	5	28	6	17	8	9	32	5	*	30	391
3 or 4	825	68	3	18	12	39	3	37	6	32	3	28	1	14	20	38	1	8	34	7	24	7	13	42	6	1	14	478
5 or more	626	68	2	19	13	41	4	39	9	33	5	27	1	11	19	31	*	6	40	7	27	11	10	45	6	*	13	495
Family composition:																												
Adults only	1151	52	4	14	8	32	3	28	5	26	4	24	1	11	14	31	1	6	28	6	18	8	10	32	5	*	28	397
Children	1338	68	3	18	12	41	4	39	7	33	4	28	1	12	19	39	1	7	37	7	25	9	2	44	6	*	14	489

* Less than 1 percent

Questions 22 and 23: "...In the past 12 months did you or did you not use any regular blankets?" "What fibers were your regular blankets made of?" (Asked only if used regular blankets in the 12 months prior to interviewing.)

	Cases	Did not use regular blankets	Used regular blankets							
			All wool	All cotton	All synthetic	Cotton and synthetic blend	Wool and cotton blend	Other	Don't know, no answer	Total fibers
	Number		Percent							
U.S. total	2489	11	40	44	33	4	2	3	14	127
Community size:										
Metropolitan	846	10	52	36	35	3	2	3	12	131
Urban	746	12	38	43	34	4	2	3	16	123
Rural	897	11	31	54	30	5	3	4	13	126
Homemaker's education:										
8th grade or less	509	8	41	55	20	3	3	2	11	123
High school - 1-3 years	493	12	29	48	29	5	3	3	14	118
High school - 4 years	909	11	40	41	37	4	2	3	15	127
College - 1-3 years	346	12	48	37	41	5	3	3	14	138
College - over 3 years	220	10	51	33	43	*	1	5	13	134
Region:										
Northeast	713	7	52	43	31	4	3	3	10	135
North Central	735	9	35	51	36	4	3	3	11	132
South	684	16	28	45	24	4	2	2	20	105
West	357	12	52	32	46	4	1	5	14	140
Homemaker's age:										
Under 30	515	11	31	39	37	4	1	4	16	116
30 - 39	523	11	39	44	41	3	2	2	14	132
40 - 49	505	13	40	42	37	4	2	4	15	129
50 - 59	404	11	43	45	29	6	3	3	14	129
60 and over	538	8	49	51	20	3	4	2	10	129
Family income:										
Lower	822	9	38	52	23	4	4	2	12	124
Middle	731	11	37	41	35	5	2	4	15	125
Upper	722	12	42	39	45	3	1	3	14	133
Family size:										
1 or 2	1038	12	42	44	25	3	3	3	15	120
3 or 4	825	11	38	40	38	4	1	4	14	125
5 or more	626	8	41	51	41	4	2	3	11	141
Family composition:										
Adults only	1151	12	43	43	25	3	3	3	15	121
Children	1338	10	38	46	40	4	2	3	13	132

* Less than 1 percent

46

Questions 22 and 23: "...In the past 12 months did you or did you not use any thermal blankets?" "What fibers were your thermal blankets made of?" (Asked only if used thermal blankets in the 12 months prior to interviewing.)

	Cases	Did not use thermal blankets	Used thermal blankets						
			All wool	All cotton	All synthetic	Cotton and synthetic blend	Other	Don't know, no answer	Total fibers
	Number	Percent							
U.S. total	2489	62	1	13	16	2	1	6	33
Community size:									
Metropolitan	846	67	2	11	14	1	1	5	28
Urban	746	59	1	14	18	1	1	7	36
Rural	897	60	2	14	16	2	1	5	36
Homemaker's education:									
8th grade or less	509	79	*	9	8	1	1	3	19
High school - 1-3 years	493	61	1	14	15	2	1	6	33
High school - 4 years	909	57	2	14	19	2	1	7	38
College - 1-3 years	346	53	1	14	21	3	2	8	41
College - over 3 years	220	59	1	18	17	1	1	6	38
Region:									
Northeast	713	65	2	12	15	1	1	5	31
North Central	735	57	1	16	18	1	1	7	38
South	684	66	1	13	14	2	1	5	30
West	357	61	1	11	18	3	1	6	34
Homemaker's age:									
Under 30	515	55	1	15	21	2	1	8	39
30 - 39	523	60	2	14	16	2	2	7	35
40 - 49	505	60	1	16	17	2	1	5	37
50 - 59	404	64	2	12	14	3	*	6	31
60 and over	538	73	2	9	12	*	1	4	24
Family income:									
Lower	822	72	1	10	11	1	1	4	24
Middle	731	59	1	14	18	2	1	7	36
Upper	722	53	2	17	21	1	1	7	42
Family size:									
1 or 2	1038	68	1	10	14	2	1	5	28
3 or 4	825	58	2	15	17	2	1	7	36
5 or more	626	58	1	15	19	2	1	6	38
Family composition:									
Adults only	1151	67	1	11	14	2	1	5	29
Children	1338	58	1	15	18	2	1	7	37

* Less than 1 percent

Questions 22 and 23: "...In the past 12 months did you or did you not use any electric blankets
fibers were your electric blankets made of?" (Asked only if used electric blankets in the 1
prior to interviewing.)

	Cases : Number	Did not :use electric: blankets :			Used electric blank			
					Percent			
U.S. total	2489	72	4	5	14	1	1	4
Community size:								
Metropolitan	846	78	4	2	11	1	1	4
Urban	746	73	3	4	14	1	1	4
Rural	897	65	4	7	17	2	*	5
Homemaker's education:								
8th grade or less	509	81	2	5	6	2	*	4
High school - 1-3 years	493	73	3	5	13	1	1	4
High school - 4 years	909	71	4	4	15	1	*	4
College - 1-3 years	346	67	5	4	19	1	1	4
College - over 3 years	220	62	7	5	20	1	*	5
Region:								
Northeast	713	82	4	2	7	1	*	4
North Central	735	78	2	5	10	1	*	3
South	684	64	3	8	19	1	1	6
West	357	55	7	4	27	2	1	4
Homemaker's age:								
Under 30	515	77	3	3	13	1	1	3
30 - 39	523	76	3	4	14	*	*	3
40 - 49	505	71	3	6	15	2	*	4
50 - 59	404	70	4	5	14	2	*	5
60 and over	538	66	5	7	13	1	1	6
Family income:								
Lower	822	76	3	6	10	1	1	4
Middle	731	71	4	4	14	2	1	5
Upper	722	69	4	4	17	1	1	4
Family size:								
1 or 2	1038	68	5	5	14	1	1	6
3 or 4	825	72	3	4	15	2	*	4
5 or more	626	78	2	5	12	*	*	3
Family composition:								
Adults only	1151	69	5	5	14	2	1	5
Children	1338	75	3	4	14	1	*	3

* Less than 1 percent

48

Questions 24, 25, and 26: "...Have you or have you not used any bedspreads in your home in the past 12 months?" "Have you or have you not used chenille or tufted bedspreads in tne past 12 months?" (Asked only if used bedspreads in the 12 months prior to interviewing.) "What fibers are they made of?" (Asked only if used chenille or tufted bedspreads in the 12 months prior to interviewing.)

	Cases	Did not use any bedspreads	Did not use chenille bedspreads	Used chenille bedspreads	Cotton	Cotton blends	Rayon/acetate	Other natural fibers	Other synthetic fibers	All other	Total fibers	Don't know, no answer
	Number						Percent					
U.S. total	2489	4	27	69	63	4	*	*	1	*	69	2
Community size:												
Metropolitan	846	6	34	60	55	3	1	1	1	1	61	2
Urban	746	3	26	71	65	3	*	-	*	*	70	2
Rural	897	3	22	75	71	5	-	-	*	*	75	1
Homemaker's education:												
8th grade or less	509	8	15	77	72	3	-	-	1	1	76	2
High school - 1-3 years	493	3	23	74	69	3	*	*	*	*	74	2
High school - 4 years	909	3	29	68	62	4	*	*	1	*	67	1
College - 1-3 years	346	5	33	62	58	4	-	1	1	1	63	1
College - over 3 years	220	3	44	53	48	5	*	-	-	-	54	*
Region:												
Northeast	713	6	25	69	62	2	*	1	1	1	67	3
North Central	735	5	24	71	66	3	*	*	1	*	71	1
South	684	2	27	71	66	5	*	-	*	*	72	*
West	357	4	36	59	56	5	-	-	1	x	61	1
Homemaker's age:												
Under 30	515	5	37	59	53	2	*	-	*	*	57	3
30 - 39	523	3	27	70	64	5	*	*	1	*	71	2
40 - 49	505	4	23	73	66	6	*	*	1	*	73	2
50 - 59	404	4	25	71	67	4	-	*	*	-	72	1
60 and over	538	5	24	71	67	2	*	1	1	1	72	1
Family income:												
Lower	822	6	22	72	68	2	*	*	*	*	72	2
Middle	731	3	25	71	66	6	*	-	*	*	72	1
Upper	722	2	34	63	57	3	*	*	1	*	63	2
Family size:												
1 or 2	1038	6	27	67	62	3	*	*	*	*	66	1
3 or 4	825	3	29	67	61	4	*	*	*	*	66	2
5 or more	626	2	24	74	68	5	*	1	1	*	76	1
Family composition:												
Adults only	1151	6	27	68	64	2	*	*	*	*	68	1
Children	1338	3	27	70	63	5	*	*	1	*	70	2

* Less than 1 percent

Questions 24, 27, and 28: "...Have you or have you not used any bedspreads in your home in th past 12 months?" "...Have you or have you not used woven bedspreads in the past 12 month (Asked only if used bedspreads in the 12 months prior to interviewing.) "What fibers are they made of?" (Asked only if used woven bedspreads in the 12 months prior to interviewi

	Cases	Did not use any bedspreads	Did not use woven bedspreads	Used woven bedspreads	Cotton	Cotton blends	Rayon/acetate	Other natural fibers	Other synthetic fibers	All other	Total fibers
	Number						Percent				
U.S. total	2489	4	61	35	27	5	1	*	1	1	34
Community size:											
Metropolitan	846	6	63	31	22	5	1	*	1	*	30
Urban	746	3	61	35	27	5	*	*	1	1	35
Rural	897	3	59	38	30	5	1	*	*	1	37
Homemaker's education:											
8th grade or less	509	8	69	23	17	3	1	*	-	1	22
High school – 1-3 years	493	3	64	33	26	4	1	*	1	*	32
High school – 4 years	909	3	60	37	29	5	*	*	1	1	36
College – 1-3 years	346	5	54	41	32	8	*	-	1	1	41
College – over 3 years	220	3	52	45	34	6	*	*	2	1	44
Region:											
Northeast	713	6	63	31	24	5	1	*	1	1	30
North Central	735	5	61	34	27	3	*	*	1	1	33
South	684	2	61	37	29	6	1	*	1	1	37
West	357	4	57	39	27	7	1	-	1	1	36
Homemaker's age:											
Under 30	515	5	63	33	23	5	*	*	1	1	30
30 – 39	523	3	60	37	28	6	1	*	1	1	37
40 – 49	505	4	56	40	30	7	1	*	1	1	40
50 – 59	404	4	61	34	27	4	*	-	*	1	34
60 and over	538	5	65	30	24	3	1	*	*	*	28
Family income:											
Lower	822	6	65	29	23	3	1	*	*	*	27
Middle	731	3	62	35	26	6	1	*	1	1	35
Upper	722	2	56	42	32	6	*	*	1	1	40
Family size:											
1 or 2	1038	6	63	31	24	3	1	*	*	1	30
3 or 4	825	3	60	37	27	5	1	*	1	1	35
5 or more	626	2	59	39	30	7	*	-	1	1	39
Family composition:											
Adults only	1151	6	63	31	24	3	*	*	*	1	30
Children	1338	3	59	38	29	5	1	*	1	1	37

* Less than 1 percent

Questions 24, 29, and 30: "...Have you or have you not used any bedspreads in your home in the past 12 months?" "Have you or have you not used tailored bedspreads in the past 12 months?" (Asked only if used bedspreads in the 12 months prior to interviewing.) "What fibers are they made of?" (Asked only if used tailored bedspreads in the 12 months prior to interviewing.)

	Cases	Did not use any bedspreads	Did not use tailored bedspreads	Used tailored bedspreads	Cotton	Cotton blends	Rayon/acetate	Other natural fibers	Other synthetic fibers	All other	Total fibers	Don't know, no answer
	Number						Percent					
U.S. total	2489	4	49	47	24	8	8	2	5	4	51	1
Community size:												
Metropolitan	846	6	40	54	27	7	10	3	6	5	59	1
Urban	746	3	45	51	26	9	10	1	5	4	55	2
Rural	897	3	59	38	20	6	6	1	3	1	38	*
Homemaker's education:												
8th grade or less	509	8	65	27	14	3	6	1	2	1	26	1
High school - 1-3 years	493	3	51	46	22	6	10	2	6	3	51	1
High school - 4 years	909	3	44	53	28	10	8	2	6	4	57	1
College - 1-3 years	346	5	38	57	30	7	12	1	6	5	62	1
College - over 3 years	220	3	38	59	30	13	6	3	5	5	62	1
Region:												
Northeast	713	6	49	45	23	5	9	2	6	3	47	1
North Central	735	5	48	47	25	10	6	2	5	4	50	1
South	684	2	53	45	24	7	9	2	2	3	48	1
West	357	4	39	57	26	11	12	2	9	3	63	1
Homemaker's age:												
Under 30	515	5	45	50	25	9	9	2	4	2	53	2
30 - 39	523	3	44	53	30	7	8	1	7	4	58	1
40 - 49	505	4	43	53	27	10	10	2	7	4	58	1
50 - 59	404	4	51	44	21	7	8	1	5	4	48	1
60 and over	538	5	59	36	18	4	7	2	3	3	37	1
Family income:												
Lower	822	6	63	31	18	4	5	1	2	2	32	1
Middle	731	3	48	48	25	9	8	2	4	4	52	1
Upper	722	2	34	64	31	12	11	2	8	5	71	1
Family size:												
1 or 2	1038	6	54	41	20	5	8	2	3	3	42	1
3 or 4	825	3	44	52	27	8	10	2	7	4	56	2
5 or more	626	2	46	52	28	11	7	2	6	4	57	1
Family composition:												
Adults only	1151	6	53	41	20	5	8	2	4	3	43	1
Children	1338	3	45	52	28	9	9	2	5	4	57	1

* Less than 1 percent

Question 31: "Let's talk about the cotton (chenille), (woven), (tailored) bed
In your opinion, what are the advantages of such a bedspread?" (Asked only
used cotton (chenille), (woven), (tailored) bedspreads in the 12 months pri
interviewing.)

	U.S. total		
	Cotton chenille	Cotton woven	
		-Percent-	
Percentage asked this question	63	27	
Care and laundering	55	20	
Easy to wash	22	7	6
Requires little or no ironing	14	5	3
Can be washed	13	6	6
Looks good after laundering	12	4	2
Easy to dry	9	2	2
Machine washable	5	1	1
Can machine dry	4	1	1
Easy to remove stains	2	1	1
Can be bleached	2	*	*
Easy to care for	2	1	1
Other	2	1	1
Performance and durability	31	17	
Lasts a long time	18	8	5
Colors stay like new	8	6	3
Does not shrink	4	2	1
Does not wrinkle	4	2	1
Holds shape	3	2	1
Does not have lint	1	3	1
Other	5	3	1
Appearance	19	11	
Attractive, pretty	8	4	5
Looks good for a long time	5	3	2
Good range of colors	4	2	3
Other	3	3	3
Comfort and Weight	8	4	
Warm	3	2	1
Lightweight	2	1	1
Other	3	2	1
Inexpensive	5	1	
Good value for the money	2	1	
All other	2	1	
No advantages	1	*	
Don't know, no answer	1	*	
Total	170	74	
Number of cases	2489	2489	

* Less than 1 percent

52

Question 32: "What are the disadvantages of such a bedspread?"
(Asked only if used cotton (chenille), (woven),
(tailored) bedspreads in the 12 months prior to interviewing.)

| | U.S. total | | |
	Cotton chenille	Cotton woven	Cotton tailored
	- - - - - - - -Percent - - - - - - -		
Percentage asked this question	63	27	24
Performance and durability	31	5	6
Has lint	23	*	*
Ravels, threads pull	4	2	1
Colors do not stay like new	2	1	2
Wears out rather quickly	2	*	1
'Pills'	2	*	*
Shrinks	1	1	1
Does not resist stain or soil	1	*	.
Stretches	1	1	*
Other	1	1	2
Not easy to dry	2	1	
Difficult to handle	2	1	1
Does not launder well	1	*	
Not attractive, not pretty	1	1	1
Heavy, bulky	1	1	*
Other	5	3	3
No disadvantages	27	16	12
Don't know, no answer	1	1	1
Total	78	29	25
Number of cases	2489	2489	2489

* Less than 1 percent

53

Question 33: "...As I mention different kinds of bedspreads, tell me how good a choice for you each bedspread would be if you were buying bedspreads now..."

	Polyester and cotton	Polyester	Cotton	Rayon/ acetate	Chenille	Woven	Tailored	Durable press
				—Percent—				
1- Not a very good choice for me	11	15	9	48	20	15	15	9
2-	8	12	7	18	8	8	10	6
3-	24	23	14	17	12	21	20	14
4-	25	21	18	8	16	23	18	21
5- A very good choice for me	27	23	51	6	42	31	34	47
Mean	3.52	3.26	3.97	2.03	3.53	3.48	3.48	3.95
Did not rate	5	6	*	2	1	2	2	4
Number of cases	2489	2489	2489	2489	2489	2489	2489	2489

* Less than 1 percent

54

Questions 34 and 35: "...As I mention some fibers used in room-size rugs for bedrooms and living rooms, tell me how good a choice for you each would be if you were buying a room-size rug for your bedroom or living room now..."

	Bedroom				Living room			
	All wool	All acrylic	All cotton	All nylon	All wool	All acrylic	All cotton	All nylon
	Percent							
1- Not a very good choice for me	35	12	42	17	28	11	56	19
2-	11	7	16	9	8	7	16	10
3-	15	19	18	17	12	19	13	15
4-	12	24	11	22	13	23	6	21
5- A very good choice for me	26	34	12	32	37	34	7	33
Mean	2.82	3.64	2.33	3.45	3.23	3.65	1.90	3.41
Did not rate	2	4	2	3	2	5	2	3
Number of cases	2489	2489	2489	2489	2489	2489	2489	2489

55

Questions 36 and 37: "...Which of these ideas would be most important if you were buying area or room-size rugs for a (bedroom), (living) Any others?"

	U.S. total	
	Bedroom	Living room
	---------------Percent---------	
Looks good for a long time	68	73
Easy to care for day-to-day	68	68
Easy to remove stains	57	68
Does not 'fuzz' or shed	51	46
Good value for the money	46	45
Good in homes with children	39	41
Does not mat down or crush easily	38	44
A certain fiber, such as wool...	33	36
Good range of colors	32	36
Does not burn easily, not flammable	26	27
Little or no static electricity	23	24
Don't know, no answer	1	1
Total	483	510
Number of cases	2489	2489

Question 38: "...Which of these describe your opinions about room-size all wool rugs? Any others?"

	Cases	Easy to remove stains	Difficult to remove stains	Looks good for a long time	Does not look good for a long time	Good value for the money	Not a good value for the money	Does not 'fuzz' or shed	Tends to 'fuzz' or shed	Good range of colors	Not a good range of colors	Does not burn easily -- not flammable	Burns easily -- flammable	Easy to care for day-to-day	Difficult to care for day-to-day	Does not mat down or crush easily	Tends to mat down or crushes easily	Little or no static electricity	A lot of static electricity	Good in homes with children	Not good in homes with children	None of these	Don't know, no answer	Total
	Number													Percent										
U.S. total	2489	15	41	52	8	35	7	21	20	37	2	12	14	30	21	28	12	18	12	16	27	1	10	438
Community size:																								
Metropolitan	846	19	39	57	7	38	5	19	21	42	2	13	13	36	18	33	10	19	12	19	24	1	11	458
Urban	746	14	43	52	10	36	7	21	23	36	2	13	15	26	22	24	17	20	13	16	27	1	8	448
Rural	897	13	42	46	8	31	8	22	22	32	1	11	13	27	22	27	9	16	16	12	30	1	12	412
Homemaker's education:																								
8th grade or less	509	14	33	44	8	30	6	19	19	30	2	11	11	25	23	23	9	15	7	12	22	*	19	379
High school - 1-3 years	493	14	42	46	9	30	7	20	19	32	2	11	14	27	23	23	14	18	10	15	28	1	11	417
High school - 4 years	909	15	43	52	8	35	7	22	20	38	2	14	15	29	29	30	13	20	14	17	28	1	6	452
College - 1-3 years	346	18	46	60	7	39	7	19	23	44	2	14	12	25	32	32	13	19	17	17	30	1	8	482
College - over 3 years	220	15	44	66	6	45	7	23	23	43	3	15	12	40	16	35	11	20	15	17	27	*	8	489
Region:																								
Northeast	713	16	37	56	7	37	5	20	20	42	1	10	12	35	18	29	7	18	10	18	24	*	9	431
North Central	735	17	46	53	9	37	7	22	22	39	2	11	18	30	21	28	10	20	18	16	27	2	10	476
South	684	12	39	43	8	27	7	18	18	27	2	11	11	27	21	24	10	13	7	9	28	1	15	374
West	357	17	46	57	8	42	7	23	21	38	3	18	15	34	23	31	15	26	15	20	30	-	6	496
Homemaker's age:																								
Under 30	515	10	49	43	10	27	9	17	25	35	3	11	17	20	28	21	15	15	17	15	34	*	13	432
30 - 39	523	11	49	50	8	33	8	15	22	32	2	10	14	26	23	24	10	16	12	15	35	2	9	428
40 - 49	505	17	42	51	8	35	7	22	18	35	2	11	13	33	20	30	12	22	12	17	28	1	9	446
50 - 59	404	18	37	54	9	38	7	26	17	40	2	17	13	32	21	32	10	19	14	17	23	1	10	457
60 and over	538	21	30	60	6	42	4	24	17	41	1	13	11	38	12	34	10	20	9	15	30	1	11	432
Family income:																								
Lower	822	15	36	47	7	34	6	20	18	34	2	13	13	35	21	23	11	15	10	14	25	1	14	401
Middle	731	13	44	50	10	36	8	20	23	37	2	13	14	29	23	28	13	19	13	15	30	1	9	450
Upper	722	16	48	56	7	33	8	20	22	39	3	12	16	32	21	30	14	21	16	19	29	1	6	476
Family size:																								
1 or 2	1038	17	34	56	7	38	6	21	22	38	2	13	13	34	16	31	11	15	12	14	18	1	11	434
3 or 4	825	16	43	50	10	33	7	20	18	38	2	12	15	28	29	26	11	19	18	18	29	1	10	438
5 or more	626	11	51	47	10	32	8	18	21	33	2	12	14	24	27	26	13	26	3	13	39		10	446
Family composition:																								
Adults only	1151	17	34	56	7	38	6	22	18	39	2	13	13	35	15	31	12	19	12	14	18	1	12	431
Children	1338	13	48	48	9	33	8	20	21	35	2	12	14	25	25	26	12	18	13	17	35	1	9	444

* Less than 1 percent

57

Question 39: "Which of these describe your opinions about room-size all acrylic rugs (such as Acrilan or Creslan)? Any others?"

	Cases (Number)	Easy to remove stains	Difficult to remove stains	Looks good for a long time	Does not look good for a long time	Good value for the money	Not a good value for the money	Does not 'fuzz' or shed	Tends to 'fuzz' or shed	Good range of colors	Not a good range of colors	Does not burn easily — not flammable	Burns easily — flammable	Easy to care for day-to-day	Difficult to care for day-to-day	Does not mat down or crush easily	Tends to mat down or crush easily	Little or no static electricity	A lot of static electricity	Good in homes with children	Not good in homes with children	None of these	Don't know, no answer	Total
		Percent																						
U.S. total	2489	45	6	36	6	27	3	19	10	36	1	11	8	41	4	20	8	11	10	33	4	1	28	367
Community size:																								
Metropolitan	846	43	10	33	10	26	5	20	12	38	1	9	11	41	4	19	9	11	13	34	5	1	26	380
Urban	746	47	6	41	5	30	5	20	11	35	1	14	7	42	4	22	9	14	9	35	3	1	27	386
Rural	897	45	3	34	3	25	1	16	8	34	*	12	6	41	2	20	6	8	7	32	4	*	32	340
Homemaker's education:																								
8th grade or less	509	26	4	22	5	16	4	10	7	20	1	8	4	26	4	10	5	6	4	17	4	1	51	255
High school - 1-3 years	493	42	5	35	6	29	2	19	6	35	*	11	7	41	4	22	5	11	8	33	4	2	29	352
High school - 4 years	909	55	6	40	6	30	1	24	13	48	*	14	8	46	3	22	9	13	11	39	4	2	20	402
College - 1-3 years	346	55	8	44	9	32	4	24	13	48	*	14	12	53	3	28	12	11	14	45	4	1	16	447
College - over 3 years	220	49	10	35	6	26	4	19	13	42	2	10	10	40	5	21	14	12	16	34	4	2	24	397
Region:																								
Northeast	713	45	6	31	8	24	4	16	10	35	1	10	12	40	3	16	7	10	14	33	4	1	28	347
N rth Central	735	49	6	38	6	31	2	19	11	39	*	12	12	47	5	23	14	14	6	36	4	1	26	402
South	684	37	6	35	3	23	2	17	7	28	1	14	4	33	4	18	6	8	12	26	4	1	35	315
West	357	52	7	40	8	33	5	25	13	43	1	15	9	47	4	27	12	12	15	42	4	-	22	437
Homemaker's age:																								
Under 30	515	46	8	37	8	28	4	20	12	38	*	12	10	43	4	19	9	12	12	40	4	*	24	394
30 - 39	523	53	8	41	8	30	2	20	12	41	*	13	13	49	3	22	8	11	9	46	4	2	17	404
40 - 49	505	50	8	39	8	28	4	21	10	40	*	13	8	47	4	24	9	12	12	36	4	1	23	403
50 - 59	404	47	4	38	4	31	2	21	8	35	*	13	8	39	4	25	7	13	10	29	2	1	31	373
60 and over	538	30	4	23	5	18	3	12	6	24	1	7	6	28	3	12	7	6	6	15	5	1	47	269
Family income:																								
Lower	822	33	4	28	4	21	2	13	7	26	1	10	6	35	3	15	5	8	5	23	4	1	42	293
Middle	731	49	6	40	6	31	3	20	11	38	1	13	7	44	4	22	9	13	9	39	4	1	23	393
Upper	722	58	8	41	9	32	5	24	13	47	1	13	10	49	4	25	12	13	17	43	4	1	16	446

58

Question 40: "Which of these describe your opinions about room-size all cotton rugs? Any others?"

	Number of Cases	Easy to remove stains	Difficult to remove stains	Looks good for a long time	Does not look good for a long time	Good value for the money	Not a good value for the money	Does not 'fuzz' or shed	Tends to 'fuzz' or shed	Good range of colors	Not a good range of colors	Does not burn easily — not flammable	Burns easily — flammable	Easy to care for day-to-day	Difficult to care for day-to-day	Does not mat down or crush easily	Tends to mat down or crushes easily	Little or no static electricity	A lot of static electricity	Good in homes with children	Not good in homes with children	None of these	Don't know, no answer	Total
														Percent										
U.S. total	2489	27	21	12	36	19	19	12	19	28	2	8	13	20	24	6	30	22	2	20	18	1	17	378
Community size:																								
Metropolitan	846	28	21	12	38	17	19	14	18	29	3	8	14	20	25	8	30	23	3	19	20	1	18	386
Urban	746	24	21	11	34	20	18	12	22	28	1	9	12	21	22	5	32	23	1	20	17	1	18	374
Rural	897	28	21	13	36	21	20	11	17	27	2	6	13	21	24	6	29	23	2	22	18	1	15	374
Homemaker's education:																								
8th grade or less	99	32	15	15	26	25	14	11	14	25	4	9	9	24	20	9	30	16	2	17	20	2	16	356
High school – 1-3 years	93	28	19	11	35	22	19	12	20	26	2	7	13	20	23	6	31	22	1	21	17	2	16	384
High school – 4 years	99	24	22	11	34	17	14	12	16	26	2	7	14	20	23	7	30	22	3	19	18	1	16	368
College – 1-3 years	96	26	27	10	45	14	24	17	22	35	2	8	16	16	33	5	36	29	2	18	20	–	13	419
College – over 3 years	20	25	41	9	47	20	20	17	16	32	2	11	14	24	22	5	34	29	3	20	24	1	15	396
Region:																								
N rtheast	713	24	18	8	36	14	17	13	13	32	2	6	10	17	22	5	30	18	3	15	18	1	23	361
North Central	735	26	26	12	39	19	23	13	23	30	2	7	19	20	28	9	34	17	1	20	22	1	17	396
South	684	37	15	20	26	28	18	19	23	32	3	8	14	26	33	6	30	30	3	27	18	1	13	381
West	357	20	30	8	47	20	15	22	14	32	3	11	15	17	31	7	36	29	3	18	20	1	13	367
Homemaker's age:																								
Under 30	515	33	18	15	30	19	17	13	13	32	2	8	10	25	17	8	30	26	2	25	17	–	18	397
30 – 39	523	27	25	11	40	19	19	15	19	30	4	6	9	19	29	6	32	23	2	21	24	2	17	393
40 – 49	505	23	23	11	38	17	17	14	17	26	2	7	8	19	25	6	33	24	2	20	18	2	11	380
50 – 59	404	24	24	13	39	21	21	14	15	26	2	8	9	20	25	8	30	22	2	18	16	1	17	380
60 and over	538	27	17	11	33	19	19	9	22	26	2	9	15	20	22	5	26	18	3	16	20	2	12	343
Family income:																								
Lower	822	31	17	17	30	24	16	12	15	28	2	8	14	26	21	7	26	20	2	23	16	1	18	369
Middle	731	27	21	12	37	18	19	12	24	25	2	6	19	19	28	6	32	25	2	20	20	1	17	386
Upper	722	27	27	15	42	15	25	14	20	31	2	6	15	18	28	6	35	26	2	18	22	1	14	401
Family size:																								
1 or 2	1038	25	20	11	35	19	20	11	18	25	2	8	11	20	23	6	29	20	2	16	15	2	19	356
3 or 4	825	28	19	14	35	19	19	12	19	30	2	6	13	22	22	7	31	22	2	23	18	1	18	382
5 or more	626	28	25	13	39	20	18	16	20	31	2	8	16	20	27	7	32	23	2	23	24	*	13	408
Family composition:																								
Adults only	1151	25	19	10	35	18	19	11	17	25	2	8	11	20	23	6	28	19	2	15	15	2	20	348
Children	1338	29	22	14	37	19	20	14	21	31	2	8	14	21	25	7	32	19	2	24	21	1	14	404

* Less than 1 percent

Question 41: "Which of these describe your opinions about room-size all nylon rugs? Any others?"

	Cases (Number)	Easy to remove stains	Difficult to remove stains	Looks good for a long time	Does not look good for a long time	Good value for the money	Not a good value for the money	Does not 'fuzz' or shed	Tends to 'fuzz' or shed	Good range of colors	Not a good range of colors	Does not burn easily -- not flammable	Burns easily -- Flammable	Easy to care for day-to-day	Difficult to care for day-to-day	Does not mat down or crush easily	Tends to mat down or crushes easily	Little or no static electricity	A lot of static electricity	Good in homes with children	Not good in homes with children	None of these	Don't know, no answer	Total
												Percent												
U.S. total	2489	52	7	44	7	33	4	23	10	39	1	11	13	46	6	24	10	9	23	39	6	1	17	.423
Community size:																								
Metropolitan	846	46	9	37	12	28	6	22	12	38	1	9	17	42	6	21	13	8	25	35	6	1	18	413
Urban	746	54	7	49	5	37	4	25	11	42	1	14	17	47	7	27	10	11	23	39	6	1	16	445
Rural	897	56	6	45	4	35	3	22	7	37	1	12	10	50	4	26	7	7	20	41	4	*	18	415
Homemaker's education:																								
8th grade or less	509	44	5	37	3	28	2	18	7	27	1	11	8	39	4	19	6	7	11	31	5	1	33	345
High school - 1-3 years	493	52	6	44	6	35	4	24	9	41	1	12	12	46	6	23	9	8	21	36	6	1	15	421
High school - 4 years	909	57	8	46	8	34	4	24	10	42	1	11	13	50	6	26	10	10	33	41	6	1	12	448
College - 1-3 years	346	51	8	48	9	38	4	23	14	45	1	11	18	47	6	29	12	8	33	41	6	-	13	462
College - over 3 years	220	56	10	42	10	33	7	25	10	43	2	13	15	47	5	25	14	8	26	39	5	*	14	451
Region:																								
Northeast	713	44	9	36	10	25	5	18	10	35	1	9	11	41	8	18	10	7	20	33	6	1	20	375
North Central	735	55	6	45	7	40	4	28	11	44	1	13	15	48	5	30	9	13	26	41	5	1	16	463
S utb	684	52	7	46	4	32	4	19	8	34	1	11	7	43	6	21	9	5	15	37	5	1	18	383
West	357	62	7	52	8	40	4	29	13	45	1	14	20	50	4	33	12	11	36	47	6	-	12	505
Homemaker's age:																								
Under 30	515	52	10	47	6	34	3	25	12	45	1	11	18	45	7	25	9	10	26	49	7	*	4	457
30 - 39	523	58	7	51	7	31	5	21	11	41	1	13	13	49	5	25	9	9	28	46	6	1	10	449
40 - 49	505	55	9	40	9	37	5	23	11	39	1	12	11	49	5	25	13	9	25	40	6		13	441
50 - 59	404	52	6	42	7	34	4	25	10	37	*	12	11	45	6	23	7	10	21	33	5	1	20	413
60 and over	538	44	5	39	5	33	3	20	5	33	1	8	10	47	4	24	7	7	13	25	4	-	30	360
Family income:																								
Lower	822	45	5	41	4	28	3	18	7	32	1	10	10	43	5	21	7	7	16	33	6	*	26	367
Middle	731	56	9	47	8	39	5	26	12	41	1	15	15	48	6	26	10	11	24	44	5	1	13	459
Upper	722	60	8	46	10	36	6	26	14	44	1	14	14	50	6	29	13	9	32	43	5	*	10	475
Family size:																								
1 or 2	1038	47	6	41	7	30	4	21	8	35	1	11	12	42	5	23	9	8	19	28	4	1	24	385
3 or 4	825	53	10	43	8	36	4	24	12	44	1	13	13	46	7	25	12	8	26	44	6	*	14	445
5 or more	626	60	7	49	6	35	4	24	12	40	1	12	13	54	5	26	8	10	26	49	6	*	11	459
Family composition:																								
Adults only	1151	47	6	39	7	31	4	22	8	35	1	11	12	42	5	23	9	8	19	28	4	1	24	383
Children	1338	57	9	47	7	35	5	24	12	43	1	12	13	54	6	25	10	9	26	48	7	*	12	458

* Less than 1 percent

Questions 42 and 43: "Have you or have you not used area or room-size rugs — NOT wall-to-wall — in any room in your home in the past 12 months?" "Let's talk about the room-size rug you purchased most recently. In which room would that be?" (Asked only if used area rugs in the 12 months prior to interviewing.)

	Cases	Did not use area rugs	Gift, never purchased	Total	Living room	Dining room	Bedroom(s)	Den, recreation room	Other
	Number			Percent					
U.S. total	2489	50	8	43	23	5	14	4	1
Community size:									
Metropolitan	846	50	7	43	22	6	16	5	1
Mn	746	44	7	48	26	5	15	4	1
Rural	897	54	9	37	23	5	10	3	*
Homemaker's education:									
8th grade or less	509	60	8	31	23	4	7	2	1
High school – 1-3 years	493	53	7	40	26	3	11	3	1
High school – 4 years	909	48	7	45	24	7	14	5	1
College – 1-3 years	346	39	9	51	22	6	21	7	1
College – over 3 years	220	40	9	51	19	8	18	10	1
Region:									
Northeast	713	39	7	54	34	8	15	4	1
N rth Central	735	51	10	39	21	6	11	4	1
South	684	59	6	34	18	3	12	5	1
West	357	49	9	42	18	4	18	6	1
Homemaker's age:									
Under 30	515	47	12	41	26	3	13	3	*
30 – 39	523	50	7	44	22	6	15	6	1
40 – 49	505	52	6	42	19	4	15	7	1
50 – 59	404	53	6	41	19	7	15	4	1
60 and over	538	47	8	44	30	8	11	2	1
Family income:									
Lower	822	56	9	34	25	4	9	1	*
Middle	731	46	9	46	26	6	15	4	1
Upper	722	45	5	50	19	7	19	8	2
Family size:									
1 or 2	1038	50	9	41	26	6	11	4	1
3 or 4	825	49	8	43	23	6	15	5	*
5 or more	626	50	6	44	20	5	17	5	1
Family composition:									
Adults only	1151	49	8	42	26	6	12	4	1
Children	1338	50	7	43	22	5	15	5	1

* Less than 1 percent

61

Question 44: "In what year did you buy the rug you purchased most recently?" (Asked only if used area rugs in the 12 months prior to interviewing.)

	Cases	Percent asked	1 year ago or less	2 years ago	3 years ago	4-5 years ago	6-10 years ago	11-15 years ago	16-20 years ago	Over 20 years ago	Don't know, no answer
	Number					Percent					
U.S. total	2489	43	7	7	6	7	8	3	1	2	2
Community size:											
Metropolitan	846	43	7	9	6	7	7	3	1	2	2
Urban	746	48	10	6	7	7	10	4	1	2	2
Rural	897	37	6	6	5	6	7	2	1	2	2
Homemaker's education:											
8th grade or less	509	31	4	6	4	5	4	3	1	2	1
High school - 1-3 years	493	40	8	6	6	6	7	3	1	1	1
High school - 4 years	909	45	7	8	7	6	9	3	*	2	2
College - 1-3 years	346	51	11	6	7	8	10	3	1	3	3
College - over 3 years	220	51	8	8	6	11	10	2	1	2	3
Region:											
Northeast	713	54	9	8	7	10	10	5	1	3	2
North Central	735	39	6	6	6	6	8	2	1	2	2
South	684	34	7	7	6	4	5	2	1	1	2
West	357	42	8	8	5	6	8	2	*	3	1
Homemaker's age:											
Under 30	515	41	15	10	7	4	3	–	*	*	1
30 - 39	523	44	8	8	7	9	9	2	*	–	1
40 - 49	505	42	6	6	8	8	9	2	1	1	2
50 - 59	404	41	4	8	6	6	9	4	1	2	1
60 and over	538	44	3	4	4	6	10	7	2	6	3
Family income:											
Lower	822	34	6	6	5	4	6	3	1	2	2
Middle	731	46	8	8	7	9	9	3	1	2	1
Upper	722	50	9	8	8	8	9	2	1	2	2
Family size:											
1 or 2	1038	41	6	5	5	6	8	4	2	4	2
3 or 4	825	43	8	8	7	6	9	2	*	1	1
5 or more	626	44	9	9	7	8	7	2	*	*	2
Family composition:											
Adults only	1151	42	6	5	4	7	8	4	2	4	2
Children	1338	43	9	9	8	7	7	2	*	*	1

* Less than 1 percent

Questions 48 and 49: "As I mention different kinds of throw or scatter rugs, tell me how good a choice for you each rug would be if you were buying throw or scatter rugs for your (bedroom), (bathroom) now."

Bedroom

	All Rayon	All Nylon	All Cotton	All Acrylic	All Wool
	- - - - - - - - - - Percent - - - - - - - - -
1- Not a very good choice for me	48	18	27	14	48
2-	16	9	12	7	9
3-	19	16	18	21	13
4-	10	24	15	22	9
5- A very good choice for me	5	31	28	32	20
Mean	2.05	3.43	3.06	3.53	2.42
Did not rate	3	3	1	4	2
Number of cases	2489	2489	2489	2489	2489

Bathroom

	All Rayon	All Nylon	All Cotton	All Acrylic	All Wool
	- - - - - - - - - - Percent - - - - - - - - -
1- Not a very good choice for me	50	19	15	17	80
2-	15	9	7	9	7
3-	17	16	14	19	5
4-	9	22	19	20	3
5- A very good choice for me	5	31	44	31	4
Mean	2.01	3.38	3.72	3.40	1.41
Did not rate	3	2	1	4	2
Number of cases	2489	2489	2489	2489	2489

Question 50: "...What advantages, if any, are there in using all cotton s
there any others?"

| | U.S. total |
	Percent
Care and laundering	79
Easy to wash	33
Can be washed	25
Machine washable	13
Easy to dry	9
Easy to remove stains	7
Looks good after laundering	5
Can machine dry	5
Easy to care for	2
Can be bleached	2
Easy to handle	2
Can be dyed or tinted	1
Performance and durability	32
Lasts a long time	13
Colors stay like new	9
Protects larger rugs or floors	4
Absorbent	3
Does not slide	3
Does not shrink	2
Resists stain or soil	1
Does not have lint	1
Holds shape	1
Other	3
Appearance	15
Good range of colors	10
Attractive, pretty	4
Looks good for a long time	2
Looks neat, fresh	1
Other	1
Comfort and weight	5
Soft	2
Warm	2
Lightweight	1
Other	1
Inexpensive	12
Good value for the money	1
All other	2
No advantages	9
Total	193
Number of cases	2489

s, if any, are there in using all cotton scatter
Are there any others?"

	U.S. total
	Percent
Performance and durability	58
Tends to slide	19
Wears out rather quickly	12
Does not lay flat or smooth	12
Colors do not stay like new	11
Has lint	9
Does not resist stain or soil	8
Tends to mat down	7
The backing disintegrates	5
Loses body, gets flimsy	2
Ravels, threads pull	2
Shrinks	2
Does not hold shape	2
Wrinkles easily	1
'Pills'	1
Flammable	1
Other	1
Appearance	
Not attractive, not pretty	4
Does not look good for a long time	3
Other	1
Care and laundering	5
Not easy to dry	4
Difficult to remove stains	2
Difficult to care for	1
Does not launder well	1
Not easy to wash	1
Other	1
Comfort and weight	3
Too light in weight	2
Other	1
All other	1
No disadvantages	31
Don't know, no answer	5
Total	152
Number of cases	2489

65

Questions 52 and 53: "Have you or have you not used any throw or scatter rugs -- rugs which are no larger than about 4' by 6' in your home in the past 12 months?" "In what rooms in your home have you used such rugs? Any others?" (Asked only if used throw or scatter rugs in the 12 months prior to interviewing.)

	Cases	Did not use	Living room	Dining room	Living/dining combination	Kitchen	Bedroom(s)	Bathroom(s)	Den, recreation room	Foyer, hall	Other	Total
	Number					Room used in — Percent						
U.S. total	2489	20	35	9	4	30	51	62	6	18	2	217
Community size:												
Metropolitan	846	24	22	6	3	25	41	60	6	20	1	183
Urban	746	20	35	8	4	30	52	61	6	15	3	214
Rural	897	16	47	12	4	36	60	65	6	19	3	252
Homemaker's education:												
8th grade or less	509	30	39	8	3	22	47	47	3	11	1	181
High school – 1-3 years	493	18	40	12	5	31	57	64	5	18	2	234
High school – 4 years	909	16	34	9	3	36	52	68	7	20	3	233
College – 1-3 years	346	17	26	7	5	30	51	64	7	19	1	211
College – over 3 years	220	19	29	7	5	23	48	65	10	21	3	210
Region:												
Northeast	713	26	24	8	2	25	46	59	6	19	1	190
N rtb Central	735	13	45	13	5	44	59	66	7	25	3	267
S utb	684	24	36	5	4	21	49	55	5	11	1	187
West	357	12	32	9	5	31	49	73	7	15	6	226
Homemaker's age:												
Under 30	515	18	34	7	4	36	50	65	4	17	2	220
30 – 39	523	19	30	6	2	32	48	66	9	18	3	214
40 – 49	505	18	34	9	3	31	54	63	9	20	2	224
50 – 59	404	21	38	11	5	26	53	60	6	17	3	221
60 ad over	538	23	39	12	4	26	51	55	3	18	1	209
Family income:												
Lower	822	27	40	9	4	26	52	55	1	13	1	201

Question 54: "...In the past 12 months did you or did you not use any draperies in any of your bedrooms? The kitchen? The living room?"

	Cases	: Did not use : any draperies	Used draperies			
			bedrooms	kitchen	living room	Total
	Number	Percent				
U.S. total	2489	20	55	14	76	146
Community size:						
Metropolitan	846	20	56	16	76	147
Urban	746	16	64	16	80	159
Rural	897	23	48	11	74	133
Homemaker's education:						
8th grade or less	509	36	38	6	61	105
High school - 1-3 years	493	20	52	12	76	141
High school - 4 years	909	13	64	17	84	165
College - 1-3 years	346	15	62	19	79	161
College - over 3 years	220	16	57	15	77	150
Region:						
Northeast	713	27	52	13	69	134
North Central	735	15	57	14	81	153
South	684	21	54	13	75	142
West	357	12	63	17	84	163
Homemaker's age:						
Under 30	515	20	53	11	74	138
30 - 39	523	16	61	19	79	159
40 - 49	505	13	64	18	84	166
50 - 59	404	17	58	11	80	149
60 and over	538	31	42	11	66	119
Family income:						
Lower	822	33	42	9	63	114
Middle	731	15	57	14	82	153
Upper	722	10	69	19	85	173
Family size:						
1 or 2	1038	25	48	13	72	133
3 or 4	825	18	60	14	78	153
5 or more	626	13	62	15	81	158
Family composition:						
Adults only	1151	24	50	13	72	135
Children	1338	16	60	15	80	155

Question 55: "What fibers are the living room draperies you used in the past 12 months made of?" (Asked only if used draperies in the living room in the 12 months prior to interviewing)

	Cases	Percent asked	Fiberglas	Cotton	Cotton and rayon/acetate	Rayon/acetate	Other synthetic	Cotton blend unspecified	Nylon	Cotton and synthetic blend	All other	Don't know, no answer
	Number						—Percent—					
U.S. total	2489	76	23	13	10	5	5	3	2	2	6	8
Community size:												
Metropolitan	846	76	23	12	9	6	5	2	2	2	7	9
Urban	746	80	26	13	12	4	4	3	1	3	5	9
Rural	897	74	22	15	10	5	6	3	2	2	5	5
Homemaker's education:												
8th grade or less	509	61	23	12	5	5	4	1	1	1	2	8
High school - 1-3 years	493	76	28	14	10	4	4	2	2	3	3	9
High school - 4 years	909	84	27	14	11	6	6	3	2	3	7	7
College - 1-3 years	346	79	16	14	14	6	6	4	1	3	8	8
College - over 3 years	220	77	14	14	12	5	5	4	2	2	10	9
Region:												
Northeast	713	69	34	10	5	5	3	1	1	1	5	5
North Central	735	81	25	15	10	5	5	3	3	2	7	8
South	684	75	17	15	10	4	7	3	1	4	6	8
West	357	84	10	15	19	9	8	4	1	1	5	11
Homemaker's age:												
Under 30	515	74	24	10	8	5	4	4	2	2	4	10
30 - 39	523	79	24	15	10	5	6	3	1	2	8	7
40 - 49	505	84	26	13	14	5	7	3	2	2	7	7
50 - 59	404	80	25	16	12	8	3	1	2	2	6	7
60 and over	538	66	19	14	8	5	5	1	1	2	4	7
Family income:												
Lower	822	63	22	13	7	4	5	3	1	2	2	6
Middle	731	82	28	16	12	6	5	3	1	3	5	7
Upper	722	85	21	13	13	6	6	3	2	2	10	10
Family size:												
1 or 2	1038	72	20	14	10	5	5	2	2	3	5	8
3 or 4	825	78	27	12	9	5	6	2	1	2	6	8
5 or more	626	81	25	14	12	6	6	4	2	1	7	6
Family composition:												
Adults only	1151	72	21	14	10	6	5	2	2	3	5	8
Children	1338	80	26	13	11	5	6	3	2	2	7	8

Question 56: "As I mention some fibers used in living room draperies, please tell me how good a choice for you each would be if you were buying draperies for your living room now. As before, select a number from 1 to 5."

	Cotton	Rayon/acetate	Cotton and rayon	Fiberglas
			Percent	
1- Not a very good choice for me	33	37	22	21
2-	12	17	15	6
3-	16	22	25	9
4-	13	13	21	15
5- A very good choice for me	24	10	15	47
Mean	2.81	2.41	2.92	3.62
Did not rate	2	2	2	3
Number of cases	2489	2489	2489	2489

69

Question 57: "In the past 12 months did you or did you not use any curtains in bedrooms? The kitchen? The living room?"

	Cases	:Did not use : :any curtains	Used curtains :Bedroom	:Kitchen	:Living room:	To
	Number------------------Percent------------------					
U.S. total	2489	11	63	80	34	1
Community size:						
Metropolitan	846	15	63	76	35	1
Urban	746	11	58	81	32	1
Rural	897	9	68	83	36	1
Homemaker's education:						
8th grade or less	509	10	65	84	42	1
High school − 1-3 years	493	9	65	82	35	1
High school − 4 years	909	11	61	80	32	1
College − 1-3 years	346	14	65	76	34	1
College − over 3 years	220	18	65	70	27	1
Region:						
Northeast	713	9	67	83	47	1
North Central	735	10	64	82	31	1
South	684	13	62	78	29	1
West	357	15	58	74	27	1
Homemaker's age:						
Under 30	515	11	66	82	34	1
30 − 39	523	12	66	78	32	1
40 − 49	505	11	59	79	30	1
50 − 59	404	11	59	83	33	1
60 and over	538	12	65	78	43	1
Family income:						
Lower	822	11	65	81	41	1
Middle	731	11	64	81	31	1
Upper	722	12	62	79	30	1
Family size:						
1 or 2	1038	15	60	77	36	1
3 or 4	825	9	66	82	35	1
5 or more	626	9	66	83	31	1
Family composition:						
Adults only	1151	15	60	77	37	1
Children	1338	9	67	83	32	1

Question 58: "What fibers are the living room curtains you used in the past 12 months made of?" (Asked only if used curtains in the living room in the 12 months prior to interviewing)

	Cases	Percent asked	Fiberglas	Cotton	Cotton and rayon/acetate	Rayon/acetate	Other synthetic	Nylon	Cotton and synthetic blend	Polyester	All other	Don't know, no answer	Total
	Number-	-	-	-	-	-	-Percent-	-	-	-	-	-	-
U.S. total	2489	34	6	6	2	2	2	7	1	5	2	2	35
Community size:													
Metropolitan	846	35	8	6	1	2	2	8	1	5	3	2	37
Urban	746	32	7	5	1	2	1	7	1	5	2	2	32
Rural	897	36	5	8	2	2	3	7	1	5	2	2	37
Homemaker's education:													
8th grade or less	509	42	6	9	3	3	4	9	1	3	2	2	43
High school - 1-3 years	493	35	8	6	2	2	2	8	1	3	2	2	35
High school - 4 years	909	32	7	5	1	2	1	7	1	5	3	1	32
College - 1-3 years	346	34	6	6	1	1	1	8	1	6	2	2	35
College - over 3 years	220	27	5	8	2	-	1	4	-	6	1	2	29
Region:													
Northeast	713	47	13	5	1	4	2	10	1	8	3	2	48
North Central	735	31	5	5	1	2	2	6	2	5	2	2	32
South	684	29	3	10	2	1	3	6	2	1	2	2	30
West	357	27	4	5	3	1	1	7	1	3	2	1	27
Homemaker's age:													
Under 30	515	34	7	7	3	3	2	6	2	2	2	3	35
30 - 39	523	32	6	7	1	2	2	6	2	5	2	2	33
40 - 49	505	30	5	4	1	1	2	7	2	6	2	1	30
50 - 59	404	33	7	5	1	3	2	9	*	3	2	1	34
60 and over	538	43	7	8	2	3	2	10	2	7	2	2	44
Family income:													
Lower	822	41	7	10	2	3	4	9	2	4	2	2	42
Middle	731	31	7	7	1	2	1	6	1	4	2	2	32
Upper	722	30	6	3	1	2	2	7	2	6	2	2	30
Family size:													
1 or 2	1038	36	6	8	2	2	2	8	2	5	2	2	37
3 or 4	825	35	8	5	1	2	2	8	1	5	3	2	36
5 or more	626	31	6	6	*	2	3	7	2	5	3	2	32
Family composition:													
Adults only	1151	37	7	7	2	2	3	8	2	5	2	2	38
Children	1338	32	6	6	1	2	2	7	2	4	3	2	33

* Less than 1 percent

71

Question 59: "As I mention some fibers used in living room curtains, please tell me how good a choice for you each would be if you were buying curtains for your living room now..."

	Cotton	Nylon	Polyester	Cotton and polyester	Fiberglas	Rayon
				Percent		
1- Not a very good choice for me	39	18	11	14	23	45
2-	12	11	8	11	5	18
3-	15	20	18	24	10	19
4-	11	21	27	28	13	10
5- A very good choice for me	23	29	31	20	45	6
Mean	2.67	3.33	3.61	3.31	3.53	2.14
Did not rate	1	2	4	3	3	2
Number of cases	2489	2489	2489	2489	2489	2489

72

Question 60: "In your opinion, what advantages, if any, are there in using all cotton draperies or curtains?"

	U.S. total
	Percent
Care and laundering	66
Can be washed	31
Easy to wash	20
Looks good after laundering	7
Easy to iron	4
Easy to care for	4
Machine washable	3
Easy to remove stains	3
Can be ironed	2
Can be starched	2
Can be bleached	2
Easy to dry	2
Requires little or no ironing	2
Can be dyed or tinted	1
Other	1
Performance and durability	26
Lasts a long time	16
Colors stay like new	9
Holds shape	3
Does not shrink	2
Resists stain or soil	1
Does not stretch	1
Other	2
Appearance	22
Good range of colors	10
Attractive, pretty	5
Hangs well	4
Looks good for a long time	3
Looks neat, fresh	2
Other	1
Comfort and weight	4
Heavy	2
Lightweight	2
Other	1
Inexpensive	11
Good value for the money	2
All other	2
No advantages	19
Don't know, no answer	5
Total	188
Number of cases	2489

Question 61: "And what disadvantages, if any, are there in using all cc
or curtains? Are there any others?"

	U.S. total
	Percent
Care and laundering	46
Requires ironing	34
Difficult to iron	7
Requires starching	4
Not easy to wash	2
Difficult to care for	2
Not easy to dry	1
Difficult to remove stains	1
Cannot be washed	1
Does not launder well	1
Difficult to handle	1
Other	2
Performance and durability	34
Colors do not stay like new	16
Does not resist stain or soil	7
Wears out rather quickly	6
Shrinks	5
Wrinkles easily	4
Does not hold shape	2
Loses body, gets flimsy	2
Stretches	1
Loses its whiteness or color	1
Flammable	1
Other	1
Appearance	14
Not attractive, not pretty	8
Does not hang well	4
Does not look neat, fresh	1
Other	3
Too light in weight	1
Heavy, bulky	1
Too expensive	1
All other	1
No disadvantages	26
Don't know, no answer	5
Total	152
Number of cases	2489

Questions 62 and 63: "...Have you or have you not used any cloth tablecloths at everyday meals in the past 12 months?" "Have you or have you not used cloth tablecloths in the past 12 months for special occasions such as holidays or when you have guests for meals?"

	Cases :	:Everyday: only :	Have used for Special occasions only:	Both:	: Have not used cloth tablecloths
	Number			Percent	
U.S. total	2489	1	36	36	26
Community size:					
Metropolitan	846	2	38	35	26
Urban	746	1	35	39	25
Rural	897	2	37	35	27
Homemaker's education:					
8th grade or less	509	1	32	27	40
High school — 1-3 years	493	2	36	33	29
High school — 4 years	909	2	37	40	22
College — 1-3 years	346	2	38	44	16
College — over 3 years	220	*	44	36	20
Region:					
Northeast	713	1	36	40	23
North Central	735	2	39	36	23
South	684	2	34	31	33
West	357	1	38	38	23
Homemaker's age:					
Under 30	515	3	32	30	35
30 - 39	523	2	33	35	29
40 - 49	505	1	41	37	22
50 - 59	404	1	41	42	17
60 and over	538	1	36	38	25
Family income:					
Lower	822	2	30	32	36
Middle	731	1	36	39	24
Upper	722	1	44	38	17
Family size:					
1 or 2	1038	2	36	36	26
3 or 4	825	1	37	36	26
5 or more	626	1	36	36	27
Family composition:					
Adults only	1151	1	36	38	25
Children	1338	2	37	35	27

* Less than 1 percent

Question 64: "Thinking only of the cloth tablecloths -- not plastic --· in the past 12 months, what fibers are they made of?" (Asked only o who used cloth tablecloths in the 12 months prior to interviewing.)

	Cases	Percent asked	Cotton	Linen	Cotton and rayon/acetate	Cotton and polyester	Rayon/acetate	Polyester	Other cotton blends
	Number						Percent		
U.S. total	2489	74	53	22	4	3	1	1	1
Community size:									
Metropolitan	846	74	50	26	4	3	1	2	1
Urban	746	75	55	21	4	3	1	1	2
Rural	897	73	53	20	4	2	2	1	1
Homemaker's education:									
8th grade or less	509	60	46	16	2	1	1	*	*
High school - 1-3 years	493	71	51	16	4	2	1	1	2
High school - 4 years	909	78	55	23	5	4	1	1	2
College - 1-3 years	346	84	61	31	5	3	2	1	2
College - over 3 years	220	80	52	31	4	4	2	3	1
Region:									
Northeast	713	77	53	27	3	3	1	2	2
North Central	735	77	56	21	5	2	2	1	1
South	684	67	46	18	4	2	1	1	1
West	357	77	58	23	6	4	1	1	*
Homemaker's age:									
Under 30	515	65	50	12	3	3	1	*	2
30 - 39	523	71	50	17	4	3	2	2	2
40 - 49	505	78	55	23	5	4	1	3	*
50 - 59	404	83	58	25	6	3	1	1	2
60 and over	538	75	52	33	3	1	2	*	*
Family income:									
Lower	822	64	48	18	2	1	1	*	*
Middle	731	76	55	22	5	3	2	1	2
Upper	722	83	57	26	6	5	1	2	2
Family size:									
1 or 2	1038	74	51	27	3	3	2	1	1
3 or 4	825	74	54	21	4	3	1	1	1
5 or more	626	73	54	15	5	4	1	2	1
Family composition:									
Adults only	1151	75	52	28	4	3	2	1	1
Children	1338	73	53	17	4	3	1	1	1

* Less than 1 percent

Question 69: "...Which of these would be most important if you were buying a tablecloth..."

	U.S. total
	Percent
Easy to remove stains	71
Looks good without ironing	59
Resists staining	50
Lasts a long time	48
Durable press finish	46
Easy to iron	40
Can be dried in a machine	39
A certain fiber, such as cotton...	27
Total	380
Number of cases	2489

Question 70: "As I mention some fibers and finishes used in tablecloths, please tell me how good a choice for you each would be if you were buying tablecloths now..."

	Linen	Cotton	Polyester	Polyester and cotton	Cotton and rayon	Durable press	Stain/soil resistant
				----------Percent----------			
1- Not a very good choice for me	20	15	12	10	29	7	3
2-	8	10	9	9	20	3	2
3-	16	22	25	25	27	9	5
4-	15	23	26	31	14	18	15
5- A very good choice for me	40	30	22	21	7	60	73
Mean	3.49	3.43	3.38	3.46	2.47	4.24	4.56
Did not rate	1	1	5	4	3	2	2
Number of cases	2489	2489	2489	2489	2489	2489	2489

78

Questions 71, 72 and 76: "... Have you or have you not purchased any yard goods in the past 12 months?" (IF YES) "Was any of this material purchased to be made into clothing?" (IF YES) "Was any of this material purchased for items other than clothing?"

	Cases Number	Have not purchased	Have purchased			
			Total	Clothing only	Other than clothing only	Both
			Percent			
U.S. total	2489	55	45	30	3	12
Community size:						
Metropolitan	846	60	40	24	4	13
Urban	746	56	44	28	3	13
Rural	897	49	51	37	3	11
Homemaker's education:						
8th grade or less	509	67	33	22	3	7
High school – 1-3 years	493	60	40	29	2	9
High school – 4 years	909	52	48	33	2	13
College – 1-3 years	346	45	55	33	3	18
College – over 3 years	220	42	58	32	6	20
Region:						
Northeast	713	64	36	22	4	10
North Central	735	53	47	31	2	13
South	684	50	50	35	3	12
West	457	48	52	35	3	14
Homemaker's age:						
Under 30	515	50	50	31	3	16
30 – 39	523	46	54	37	2	15
40 – 49	505	50	50	34	4	12
50 – 59	404	58	42	29	2	11
60 and over	538	69	31	21	3	7
Family income:						
Lower	822	66	34	24	2	7
Middle	731	48	52	34	3	14
Upper	722	46	54	33	4	18
Family size:						
1 or 2	1038	65	35	23	3	10
3 or 4	825	51	49	32	4	14
5 or more	626	43	57	40	3	14
Family composition:						
Adults only	1151	65	35	22	3	10
Children	1338	46	54	37	3	14

79

	2489	42	35	20	11	67
U.S. total	2489	42	35	20	11	67
Community size:						
Metropolitan	846	37	30	18	10	58
Urban	746	41	34	21	10	65
Rural	897	49	41	22	13	76
Homemaker's education:						
8th grade or less	509	30	25	11	6	42
High school – 1-3 years	493	38	29	21	10	60
High school – 4 years	909	46	38	23	2	73
College – 1-3 years	346	52	45	25	15	85
College – over 3 years	220	52	46	21	16	84
Region:						
Northeast	713	32	27	13	7	47
North Central	735	44	35	23	13	70
South	684	47	41	22	10	73
West	357	49	42	27	17	86
Homemaker's age:						
Under 30	515	47	39	15	21	75
30 – 39	523	52	40	37	16	93
40 – 49	505	45	35	20	6	71
50 – 59	404	40	37	13	6	56
60 and over	538	28	26	6	4	36
Family income:						
Lower	822	32	27	2	8	47
Middle	731	48	39	24	14	78
Upper	722	51	42	28	12	83
Family size:						
1 or 2	1038	33	31	7	5	43
3 or 4	825	46	39	21	13	73
5 or more	626	54	38	41	18	97
Family composition:						
Adults only	1151	33	31	6	5	43

Questions 74 and 78: "What was the fiber content of the material you bought for (clothing), (other items)?" (Asked only if purchased material for (clothing), (other items) in the 12 months prior to interviewing.)

	U.S. total	
	Clothing	Other items
	- - - - - - Percent - - - - - -	
Percentage asked this question	42	15
Cotton	33	11
Wool	12	*
Cotton and polyester	8	1
Polyester	8	1
Rayon/acetate	3	1
All other blends	3	1
Acrylic	2	*
Nylon	2	1
Linen	2	*
Cotton blend unspecified	2	1
Cotton and rayon/acetate	2	1
Silk	2	*
Wool blends unspecified	2	
Synthetic	1	*
All other fibers	3	1
Don't know, no answer	1	*
Total	84	18
Number of cases	2489	2489

* Less than 1 percent

81

Question 75: "..How many articles of clothing have been made in the past 12 months from material you purchased?"
(Asked only if purchased material for clothing in the 12 months prior to interviewing.)

	Cases	Percent asked	1 or 2	3 to 5	6 to 10	11 to 15	16 to 25	26 and over	None	Don't know
	Number					Percent				
U.S. total	2489	42	6	9	10	6	5	5	1	*
Community size:										
Metropolitan	846	37	6	9	9	5	3	4	1	*
Urban	746	41	5	8	10	5	6	6	1	-
Rural	897	49	8	10	10	7	6	6	1	*
Homemaker's education:										
8th grade or less	509	30	5	8	5	4	3	2	2	*
High school - 1-3 years	493	38	6	8	8	4	5	6	1	*
High school - 4 years	909	46	6	10	12	7	5	6	1	*
College - 1-3 years	346	52	7	9	12	7	7	7	1	1
College - over 3 years	220	52	7	13	11	10	5	5	1	-
Region:										
Northeast	713	32	7	7	8	4	3	3	1	*
North Central	735	44	7	9	9	6	5	5	2	*
South	684	47	7	9	12	7	5	6	1	*
West	357	49	3	12	10	6	8	9	1	*
Homemaker's age:										
Under 30	515	47	9	9	11	7	5	5	1	*
30 - 39	523	52	6	11	11	8	6	9	1	*
40 - 49	505	45	5	8	10	7	7	7	1	1
50 - 59	404	40	5	11	8	6	5	3	1	*
60 and over	538	28	6	7	7	2	1	2	2	*
Family income:										
Lower	822	32	7	9	6	4	2	3	1	*
Middle	731	48	6	10	11	6	8	6	1	*
Upper	722	51	6	10	12	8	6	7	1	*

Question 77: "...Was it for --" (Asked only if purchased material for items other than clothing in the 12 months prior to interviewing.)

	Cases	Percent asked	Curtains or draperies	Slip covers, upholstery	Bedspreads, quilts	Tablecloths, table mats	Cushion covers, pillows	Pillow cases	All other	Total
	Number- - - - - - - Percent- - - - - - - - -									
U.S. total	2489	15	11	2	2	1	1	1	2	20
Community size:										
Metropolitan	846	16	11	4	2	2	1	*	2	22
Urban	746	16	11	2	2	1	2	1	2	23
Rural	897	14	10	1	2	1	1	*	2	17
Homemaker's education:										
8th grade or less	509	11	8	1	1	1	1	*	1	13
High school - 1-3 years	493	11	7	2	1	1	1	1	2	14
High school - 4 years	909	15	10	2	2	2	1	1	2	20
College - 1-3 years	346	22	17	4	4	1	1	*	3	31
College - over 3 years	220	26	17	7	4	1	1	-	3	33
Region:										
Northeast	713	14	10	4	2	1	1	-	1	19
North Central	735	16	10	2	2	2	1	1	3	23
South	684	15	11	2	2	*	1	*	1	17
West	357	17	11	2	3	2	1	1	3	23
Homemaker's age:										
Under 30	515	19	15	3	3	1	1	-	2	25
30 - 39	523	18	13	3	2	2	1	1	3	24
40 - 49	505	16	11	2	3	3	2	1	2	24
50 - 59	404	13	8	2	2	1	*	1	1	16
60 and over	538	10	5	2	2	1	1	1	1	12
Family income:										
Lower	822	10	7	1	1	*	1	1	*	11
Middle	731	17	12	3	2	2	1	1	3	23
Upper	722	21	16	4	3	3	2	1	3	30
Family size:										
1 or 2	1038	13	7	2	2	1	1	1	2	15
3 or 4	825	17	13	2	2	1	1	1	2	22
5 or more	626	17	12	4	3	2	1	*	3	25
Family composition:										
Adults only	1151	13	8	2	2	1	1	1	1	16
Children	1338	17	13	3	2	1	1	*	2	24

* Less than 1 percent

Question 79: "How many such items have been made in the past 12 months from material you purchased?" (Asked only if purchased material for items other than clothing in the 12 months prior to interviewing.)

	Cases	Percent asked	1 or 2	3 to 5	6 to 10	11 or over	None
	Number			Percent			
U.S. total	2489	15	6	4	3	1	1
Community size:							
Metropolitan	846	16	6	5	3	1	1
Urban	746	16	6	4	3	2	1
Rural	897	14	5	4	3	1	1
Homemaker's education:							
8th grade or less	509	11	3	4	2	1	1
High school - 1-3 years	493	11	4	3	2	1	1
High school - 4 years	909	15	6	4	2	2	1
College - 1-3 years	346	22	9	6	5	1	1
College - over 3 years	220	26	10	7	6	1	3
Region:							
Northeast	713	14	4	5	3	2	1
North Central	735	16	6	4	3	2	1
South	684	15	6	5	2	1	1
West	357	17	8	4	3	1	1
Homemaker's age:							
Under 30	515	19	7	7	3	2	*
30 - 39	523	18	8	4	4	1	*
40 - 49	505	16	6	5	2	2	1
50 - 59	404	13	4	3	2	2	2
60 and over	538	10	3	3	2	1	2
Family income:							
Lower	822	10	3	3	2	1	1
Middle	731	17	6	5	3	2	1
Upper	722	21	9	5	3	2	1
Family size:							
1 or 2	1038	13	4	3	3	1	1
3 or 4	825	17	7	5	3	1	1
5 or more	626	17	6	6	3	2	*
Family composition:							
Adults only	1151	13	4	3	3	1	1
Children	338	17	7	5	3	1	1

* Less than 1 percent

84

Background information: Relationship among characteristics used as standard cross tabulations 1/

Characteristic	Region				Community size			Homemaker's age				
	Northeast	North Central	South	West	Metropolitan	Urban	Rural	Under 30	30-39	40-49	50-59	60 and over
							Percent					
Region:												
Northeast	100				44	30	13	29	31	29	26	28
North Central		100			25	26	37	27	31	32	29	29
South			100		13	30	39	28	24	24	28	33
West				100	18	14	11	16	14	15	17	11
Community size:												
Metropolitan	53	28	16	42	100			39	35	37	31	28
Urban	31	27	33	29		100		29	33	31	30	27
Rural	16	45	51	29			100	33	32	32	39	45
Homemaker's age:												
Under 30	21	18	21	24	23	19	18	100				
30-39	23	22	19	20	22	23	19		100			
40-49	21	22	18	21	22	21	18			100		
50-59	15	16	16	20	15	16	18				100	
60 and over	21	21	26	16	18	20	27					100
Homemaker's education:												
Grade school	21	19	26	11	18	16	26	6	9	18	27	43
Some high school	19	20	22	17	17	23	20	21	18	20	23	18
Completed high school	37	39	33	37	35	40	35	42	47	40	32	22
Any college	22	21	19	35	30	20	18	31	26	22	17	17
Family income:												
Lower	33	27	42	27	26	30	42	30	18	19	37	60
Middle	27	30	30	30	27	32	29	27	36	31	25	16
Upper	29	33	19	38	37	30	20	28	41	38	28	11
Family size:												
1 or 2	38	43	44	42	40	41	44	25	10	26	63	87
3 or 4	38	30	31	34	36	34	30	52	32	42	29	11
5 or more	23	28	25	24	24	26	26	23	58	31	8	3
Family composition:												
Adults only	46	46	47	47	46	46	47	24	12	32	73	95
Children in household	54	54	53	53	54	54	53	76	88	68	27	5
Number of respondents	713	735	684	357	846	746	897	515	523	505	404	538

1/ Percentages may not add to 100 because some characteristics were not ascertained for some respondents or because of rounding.

Continued--

Background information: Relationship among characteristics used as standard cross tabulations 1/ -- Continued

Characteristic	Homemaker's education				Family income			Family size			Family composition	
	Grade school	Some high school	Completed high school	Any college	Lower	Middle	Upper	1 or 2	3 or 4	5 or more	Adults only	Children in household
	Percent												
Region:												
Northeast	29	27	29	28	29	27	29	26	33	27	28	29
North Central	28	30	32	27	24	30	34	30	26	32	29	30
South	35	31	25	23	35	28	18	29	26	27	28	27
West	8	12	14	22	12	15	19	14	15	14	15	14
Community size:												
Metropolitan	30	29	33	44	27	32	44	32	36	33	33	35
Urban	24	35	33	26	27	32	31	30	31	31	30	30
Rural	46	36	35	29	46	36	25	38	33	36	37	35
Homemaker's age:												
Under 30	6	22	24	28	19	26	20	12	32	18	11	29
30-39	9	19	27	24	11	26	30	5	20	49	5	35
40-49	17	20	22	20	12	22	27	13	26	25	14	26
50-59	22	19	14	12	18	14	16	24	14	5	25	8
60 and over	45	20	13	16	39	12	8	45	7	2	44	2
Homemaker's education:												
Grade school	100				41	12	6	28	15	16	28	14
Some high school		100			25	21	13	19	21	20	18	21
Completed high school			100		24	43	44	30	40	42	30	42
Any college				100	10	23	38	23	23	22	24	22
Family income:												
Lower	67	42	22	13	100			47	24	21	43	25
Middle	17	32	35	30		100		24	31	36	25	33
Upper	8	19	35	48			100	19	36	36	22	35
Family size:												
1 or 2	56	40	34	42	59	34	27	100			87	3
3 or 4	24	35	37	34	25	35	42		100		13	51
5 or more	20	25	29	24	16	31	31			100	1	46
Family composition:												
Adults only	62	43	37	48	60	40	34	96	18	1	100	
Children in household	38	57	63	52	40	60	66	4	82	99		100
Number of respondents	509	493	909	566	822	731	722	1,038	825	626	1,151	1,338

1/ Percentages may not add to 100 because some characteristics were not ascertained for some respond─ or because of rounding.

86

Bureau of Budget No. 40-S69027
Expiration Date: 12/31/69   QUESTIONNAIRE

> With the exception of check-box material, office record information,
> and free-answer space, the questionnaire used for this study is
> reproduced below in entirety. The cards used are reproduced at the
> end of the questionnaire. Instructions to interviewers and
> respondents are in upper case letter.

Good _____, I am _____ of National Analysts, Inc. We are con-
ducting a study for the United States Department of Agriculture all across the country to
learn about people's attitudes toward some of the household items available to them. Your
household has been selected to be part of this study.

1. We will be discussing household items made of fiber -- such as sheets and tablecloths --
which you have gotten for use in your home. Let's begin with bedroom furnishings --
furnishings for adult use, not for infants or small children. We'll talk first about sheets.
How long ago did you last get any sheets for use in your home -- excluding crib sheets or
sheets for youth beds?

IF ONE YEAR OR LESS RECORD EXACT WEEKS OR MONTH AND CONTINUE QUESTIONING OTHERWISE SKIP TO
QUESTION 9

2. Did you buy them or get them as a gift?

3. How many did you get at that time? ENTER EXACT NUMBER

4. In addition to these sheets, did you get any other sheets in the past 12 months?

5. How long ago did you get these other sheets? ENTER EXACT NUMBER OF MONTHS

6. Did you buy those sheets or get them as a gift?

7. How many did you get at that time? ENTER EXACT NUMBER

8. Then that makes a total of (ENTER EXACT NO. HERE) sheets that you have gotten in the past
12 months? Is that correct?

9. As you may know, sheets are generally made of all cotton or a blend of cotton and a
synthetic fiber, such as polyester. Percale and muslin are weaves, not fibers. Either weave
can be made of all cotton fiber or a blend. Permanent press -- also called durable press --
is a special finish which is used on a variety of products made of cloth.

This card (HAND RESPONDENT CARD A) lists some different kinds of fibers and finishes used for
sheets. Which of these have you used in your home in the past 12 months? Any others?

10. HAND RESPONDENT CARD B This is a scale to help people indicate their opinions. You will
notice that the top says "Five -- a very good choice for me" and the bottom says "One -- not
a very good choice for me." You can pick any of the numbers from one to five -- the better
a choice for you the higher the number you will select. With this in mind, as I mention
each kind of sheets, tell me the number that expresses your opinion of how good a choice it
would be for you if you were buying sheets now. (Even if you haven't used that kind in your
home.)

11. Now we would like to know how important some ideas would be if you were buying sheets.
(HAND RESPONDENTS CARD C) We know that all of these ideas may be important, but some are
probably more important to you than others. Please tell me which of these ideas would be
most important to you if you were buying sheets. Any others?

12. HAND RESPONDENT CARD D This card has some of the phrases on it which we just talked
about. We are interested in your opinions about different kinds of sheets, even if you have
not used them in your home. Which of these phrases describe your opinions about polyester
and cotton blend sheets? Any others? (RECORD COL. A)

13. Which of these describe your opinions about all cotton sheets? Any others? (RECORD
COL. B)

14. Which of these describe your opinions about durable or permanent press sheets made of polyester and cotton blend? Any others? (RECORD COL. C)

15. Which of these describe your opinions about durable or permanent press sheets made of all cotton? Any others? (RECORD COL. D)

16. How do you usually care for your sheets? (READ IDEAS TO RESPONDENT) 1. Have them washed and dried at a commercial laundry 2. Wash them in a machine at home or a laundermat 3. Dry them in a machine at home or a laundermat 4. Dry them on a clothesline 5. Dry on line or in machine depending on weather 0. Other (write in)

17. EVERYONE Now I would like to ask you a few questions about blankets. As I mention different kinds of blankets, tell me how good a choice for you each blanket would be if you were buying blankets now. As before, select a number from 1 to 5. (Even if you haven't used that kind in your home.) (HAND RESPONDENT CARD B)

18. HAND RESPONDENT CARD E Let's talk about how important some ideas would be if you were buying blankets. We know that all of these ideas may be important, but some are probably more important to you than others. Please tell me which of these ideas would be most important if you were buying blankets. Any others?

19. HAND RESPONDENT CARD F This card has phrases which some people think are true of different kinds of blankets. Which of these describe your opinions about all wool blankets? Any others? (RECORD IN COL. A)

20. Which of these describe your opinions about all cotton blankets? Any others? (RECORD IN COL. B)

21. Which of these describe your opinions about blankets made of an all synthetic fiber? Any others? (RECORD IN COL. C)

22. Now I'd like to know about the kinds of blankets you use. In the past twelve months did you or did you not use any regular blankets? Electric blankets? Thermal blankets? (RECORD)

23. (FOR EACH "YES" TO Q. 22) What fibers were your (TYPE) made of?

(CIRCLE THE NUMBER) 1. All wool 2. All cotton 3. All synthetic 0. Other (write in)

24. Let's turn now to another household item used in bedrooms -- namely, bedspreads. Have you or have you not used any bedspreads in your home in the past twelve months?

IF NO TO QUESTION 24 SKIP TO QUESTION 33

25. Have you or have you not used chenille or tufted bedspreads in the past twelve months?

IF NO TO QUESTION 25 SKIP TO QUESTION 27

26. What fibers are they made of?

The bedspread industry separates bedspreads into three types. In addition to the tufted or chenille bedspread, a second type is the woven. This type is made of material woven mainly for bedspreads. It is generally heavier and the pattern or color is woven through, not printed on. It has almost the same pattern on both sides except the colors are reversed. All other bedspreads are called tailored. These are made of material that could be used for other items. They may be quilted, flat or ruffled, fitted or not. 27. Have you or have you not used woven bedspreads in the past twelve months?

IF NO TO QUESTION 27 SKIP TO QUESTION 29

28. What fibers are they made of?

29. Have you or have you not used tailored bedspreads in the past twelve months?

IF NO TO QUESTION 29 SKIP TO QUESTION 31

30. What fibers are they made of?

ASK QUESTIONS 31 AND 32 IN SEQUENCE FOR EACH TYPE/FIBER USED IN Q'S 25-30

31. Let's talk about the (type/fiber) bedspread. In your opinion, what are the advantages of such a bedspread? (RECORD IN COL. A)

32. What are the disadvantages of such a bedspread? (RECORD IN COL. B)

33. HAND RESPONDENT CARD B This is the scale we used before. As I mention different kinds of bedspreads, tell me how good a choice for you each bedspread would be if you were buying bedspreads now. Again, select a number from 1 to 5. (Even if you haven't used that kind in your home.)

34. EVERYONE Now I'd like you to think about room-size rugs -- that is, larger than 4' x 6', but NOT wall-to-wall. As I mention some fibers used in room-size rugs for bedrooms, tell me how good a choice for you each would be if you were buying a room-size rug for your bedroom now. As before, select a number from 1 to 5. (Even if you haven't used that kind in your home.) (HAND RESPONDENT CARD B) (RECORD IN COL. A)

35. USING CARD B Now as I mention some fibers used in room-sized rugs -- not wall-to-wall -- for living rooms, tell me how good a choice for you each fiber would be if you were buying room-size rugs for the living room now. As before, select a number from 1-5. (Even if you haven't used that kind in your home) (RECORD IN COL. B)

36. HAND RESPONDENT CARD G Let's talk about how important some ideas would be if you were buying area or room-size rugs for a bedroom. We know that all of these ideas may be important, but some are probably more important to you than others. Please tell me which of these ideas would be most important to you if you were buying area or room-size rugs for a bedroom. Any others? (RECORD IN COL. A)

37. Please tell me which of these ideas would be most important to you if you were buying area or room-size rugs for your living room? Any others? (RECORD IN COL. B)

38. HAND RESPONDENT CARD H This card has some phrases which people think are true of some kinds of rugs. Which of these describe your opinions about room-size all wool rugs? Any others? (RECORD IN COL. A)

39. Which of these describe your opinions about room-size all acrylic rugs (such as Acrilan or Creslan)? Any others? (RECORD IN COL. B)

40. Which of these describe your opinions about room-size all cotton rugs? Any others? (RECORD IN COL. C)

41. Which of these describe your opinions about room-size all nylon rugs? Any others? (RECORD IN COL. D)

42. Have you or have you not used area or room-size rugs -- NOT wall-to-wall -- in any room in your home in the past 12 months?

IF NO TO QUESTION 42 SKIP TO QUESTION 48

43. Let's talk about the room-size rug you purchased most recently. In which room would that be? (CIRCLE THE NUMBER) 1. Living room 2. Dining room 3. Bedroom(s) 4. Den, recreation room 0. Other (write in)

IF GIFT, NEVER PURCHASED SKIP TO QUESTION 48

44. In what year did you buy the rug you purchased most recently?

YEAR: 19_____

IF MORE THAN ONE RUG PURCHASED MOST RECENTLY, ASK QUESTIONS 45-47 IN SEQUENCE ABOUT EACH. INDICATE ROOM IN WHICH USED.

45. HAND RESPONDENT CARD I Of what fiber or fibers is it made? (RECORD IN COL. A)

46. What size is it? (RECORD IN COL. B)

47. As far as you can remember, how much did you pay for your (ROOM/FIBER) i
COL. C)

48. EVERYONE Let's talk about small rugs, that is, throw or scatter rugs --
no larger than 4' x 6'. As I mention different kinds of throw or scatter ru
good a choice for you each rug would be if you were buying throw or scatter
bedroom now. As before, select a number from 1 to 5. (Even if you haven't t
your home.) (HAND RESPONDENT CARD B) (RECORD IN COL. A)

49. Now as I mention different kinds of throw or scatter rugs for the bathrc
me how good a choice for you each rug would be if you were buying throw or s
the bathroom now. As before, select a number from 1 to 5. (Even if you hav
kind in your home.) (RECORD IN COL. B)

50. Let's talk about cotton scatter or throw rugs for either room. What adv
are there in using all cotton scatter rugs? Are there any others?

51. And what disadvantages, if any, are there in using all cotton scatter ru
any others?

52. Have you or have you not used any throw or scatter rugs -- rugs which ar
about 4' by 6' in your home in the past 12 months?

IF NO TO QUESTION 52 SKIP TO QUESTION 54

53. In what rooms in your home have you used such rugs? Any others? (CIRCI
GIVEN) 1. Living room 2. Dining room 3. Living/dining combination 4.
5. Bedroom(s) 6. Bathroom(s) 7. Den, recreation room 8. Foyer, hall
in)

EVERYONE Now let's talk about draperies and curtains. Draperies are window
are frequently made of heavier materials, and are generally more "formal."
less formal window hangings which are unlined, thinner materials and often t
54. In the past 12 months did you or did you not use any draperies in any of
The kitchen? The living room?

IF "DID NOT" TO LIVING ROOM, SKIP TO Q. 56

55. What fibers are the living room draperies you used in the past 12 months
referring just to the draperies and not the linings.

56. HAND RESPONDENT CARD B As I mention some fibers used in living room dra
tell me how good a choice for you each would be if you were buying draperies
room now. As before, select a number from 1 to 5. (Even if you haven't use
your home.)

57. EVERYONE In the past 12 months did you or did you not use any curtains
The kitchen? The living room?

IF "DID NOT" TO LIVING ROOM, SKIP TO Q. 59

58. What fibers are the living room curtains you used in the past 12 months

59. HAND RESPONDENT CARD B As I mention some fibers used in living room cu
tell me how good a choice for you each would be if you were buying curtains
room now. As before, select a number from 1 to 5. (Even if you haven't use
your home.)

60. EVERYONE In your opinion, what advantages, if any, are there in using ,
or curtains? (I am referring only to the draperies themselves not to the l
any others?)

61. And what disadvantages, if any, are there in using all cotton draperies
there any others?

90

62. Now let's talk about tablecloths. We are interested in tablecloths which are made of cloth -- not plastic, paper, or plastic coated cloth. Have you or have you not used any cloth tablecloths at everyday meals in the past 12 months?

63. EVERYONE Have you or have you not used cloth tablecloths in the past 12 months for special occasions such as holidays or when you have guests for meals?

IF "HAVE NOT" TO BOTH Q. 62 AND Q. 63, SKIP TO Q. 69

64. Thinking only of the cloth tablecloths -- not plastic -- that you used in the past 12 months, what fibers are they made of? (ENTER IN COL. A)

65. Have any of these tablecloths which you used in the past 12 months had any special finishes which are supposed to make them more convenient to use or haven't they?

IF "HAVE NOT" TO QUESTION 65 SKIP TO QUESTION 69

66. (FOR EACH FIBER LISTED IN COL. A, ASK:) Do any of your (FIBER) tablecloths have a special finish? (IF "YES") What special finishes do they have -- that is, what are the finishes supposed to do? (RECORD NEXT TO PROPER FIBER IN COL. B)

(ASK QUESTIONS 67 AND 68 IN SEQUENCE FOR EACH DIFFERENT FIBER/FINISH COMBINATION RECORDED IN QUESTIONS 64 AND 66.)

67. In your opinion, what are the advantages, if any, of a (FIBER/FINISH) tablecloth? (RECORD IN COL. C)

68. What are the disadvantages, if any, of such a tablecloth? (RECORD IN COL. D)

69. HAND RESPONDENT CARD J Let's talk about how important some ideas would be if you were buying tablecloths. As before, we know that all these ideas may be important, but some are probably more important than others to you. Please tell me which of these would be most important if you were buying a tablecloth. Any others?

70. HAND RESPONDENT CARD B As I mention some fibers and finishes used in tablecloths, please tell me how good a choice for you each would be if you were buying tablecloths now. As before, select a number from 1 to 5. (Even if you haven't used that kind in your home.)

71. EVERYONE Let's turn, finally, to yard goods for home sewing. Have you or have you not purchased any yard goods in the past 12 months?

IF NO IN QUESTION 71 SKIP TO QUESTION 80

72. Was any of this material purchased to be made into clothing?

IF NO IN QUESTION 72 SKIP TO QUESTION 77

73. IF YES Was any of it to be made into clothing for -- . . . people 19 years old or older? . . . children between 6 and 18 years old? . . . children less than 6 years old?

74. What was the fiber content of the material you bought for clothing?

75. All in all, how many articles of clothing have been made in the past 12 months from material you purchased? (ENTER NUMBER)

76. Was any of this material purchased for items other than clothing?

IF NO TO QUESTION 76 SKIP TO QUESTION 80

77. (IF "YES" TO Q. 76 OR "NO" TO Q. 72) Was it for -- Bedspreads? Curtains or draperies? Something else? (write in)

78. What was the fiber content of the material you bought for these other items?

79. How many such items have been made in the past 12 months from material you purchased?

(IF "YES" TO CURTAINS OR DRAPERIES IN Q. 77, Please count a
a single item.) (ENTER NUMBER)

80. Thank you. Now when we put together all the things peo
answers from people who are alike in one or more ways. In
to put your answers, we need to know something about you an

How many people are there living in this (house) (apartment

81. How many are: Under 6 years old? 6 to 18 years old?

82. How old are you?

83. What was the last grade of school you completed? (CIRC

84. Do you own this (house) (apartment) or rent it?

85. HAND RESPONDENT CARD K (income card) And finally, whic
contains the total household income from all sources BEFORE

ENTER FROM OBSERVATION
Type of dwelling:

CARDS USED IN INTERVIEWS

CARD A--Q. 9   CARD B

Polyester and cotton blend   A very

All Cotton

Durable or permanent press sheets made of
 polyester and cotton blend

Durable or permanent press sheets made of
 all cotton

                                                  Not a

Easy to wash

Looks good without ironing

Smooth to the touch

Easy to remove stains

Can be bleached

Keeps its whiteness or color a long time

Made of a certain fiber, such as cotton, a
  polyester/cotton blend, or something else

Lasts a long time

Good value for the money

Absorbent

Can buy it on sale

A certain weave, such as muslin or percale

Does not "pill" -- does not make little "balls"

Easy to dry

Good range of colors and prints

CARD D--Q.'s 12-15

Easy to wash	Not easy to wash
Looks good without ironing	Does not look good without ironing
Rough to the touch	Smooth to the touch
Easy to remove stains	Difficult to remove stains
Must not be bleached	Can be bleached
Keeps its whiteness or color a long time	Does not keep its whiteness or color a long time
Lasts a long time	Wears out rather quickly
Not good value for the money	Good value for the money
Absorbent	Not absorbent
Can buy it on sale	Cannot buy it on sale
"Pills" -- makes little "balls"	Does not "pill" -- does not make little "balls"
Easy to dry	Not easy to dry
Not a good range of colors and prints	Good range of colors and prints

Can be washed

Easy to remove stains

Colors stay like new

Made of a certain fiber, such as cotton,
wool or a synthetic

Lasts a long time

Good value for the money

Can buy it on sale

Does not "pill" -- does not make little "balls"

Good range of colors

Does not shrink

Does not stretch

Does not burn easily -- not flammable

Good for use all year round

CARD F--Q.'s 19-21

Can be washed	Must not be washed
Difficult to remove stains	Easy to remove stains
Colors stay like new	Colors do not stay like new
Wears out rather quickly	Lasts a long time
Not good value for the money	Good value for the money
Can buy it on sale	Cannot buy it on sale
"Pills" -- makes little "balls"	Does not "pill" -- does not make little "balls"
Good range of colors	Not a good range of colors
Does not shrink	Shrinks
Does not stretch	Stretches
Burns easily -- flammable	Does not burn easily -- not flammable
Not good for use all year round	Good for use all year round

Easy to remove stains

Made of a certain fiber -- such as wool,
an acrylic, cotton, or something else

Looks good for a long time

Good value for the money

Does not "fuzz" or shed

Good range of colors

Does not burn easily, not flammable

Easy to care for on a day-to-day basis

Does not mat down or crush easily

Little or not static electricity

Good in homes where there are children

CARD H--Q.'s 38-41

Difficult to remove stains	Easy to remove stains
Does not look good for a long time	Looks good for a long time
Good value for the money	Not a good value for the money
Does not "fuzz" or shed	Tends to "fuzz" or shed
Good range of colors	Not a good range of colors
Burns easily -- flammable	Does not burn easily -- not flammable
Difficult to care for on a day-to-day basis	Easy to care for on a day-to-day basis
Does not mat down or crush easily	Tends to mat down or crushes easily
Little or no static electricity	A lot of static electricity
Not good in homes where there are children	Good in homes where there are children

CARD I--Q. 45

All wool

All acrylic
(such as Acrilan, Creslan, Orlon)

All cotton

All nylon

All rayon

All polyester
(such as Dacron, Kodel)

Wool/synthetic blend

CARD J--Q. 69

Looks good without ironing

Easy to remove stains

Made of a certain fiber, such as
cotton, polyester and cotton, linen,
rayon, or something else

Lasts a long time

Easy to iron

Resists staining

Can be dried in a machine

Durable or permanent press finish

CARD K--Q. 85

INCOME

	Weekly	Annually
1.	$19 or less	Under $1,000
2.	$20 - $57	$1,000 - $2,999
3.	$58 - $76	$3,000 - $3,999
4.	$77 - $96	$4,000 - $4,999
5.	$97 - $115	$5,000 - $5,999
6.	$116 - $134	$6,000 - $6,999
7.	$135 - $153	$7,000 - $7,999
8.	$154 - $173	$8,000 - $8,999
9.	$174 - $192	$9,000 - $9,999
10.	$193 - $211	$10,000 - $10,999
11.	$212 - $230	$11,000 - $11,999
12.	$231 - $288	$12,000 - $14,999
13.	$289 or more	$15,000 or more

96

Lightning Source UK Ltd.
Milton Keynes UK
UKHW010255231118
332756UK00012B/1945/P